Finding
your self at

# The
# Heartbreak
# Hotel

Finding
your self at

# The
# Heartbreak
# Hotel

## ALICE HADDON
## RUTH FIELD

*To our mums –*

*Tessa Haddon (1938-2020)*

*and Kay Field*

# Contents

**Part II: The Future**

## The Sun

*She saw herself like a small creature*

*Laying in the sun, needing to keep warm to sustain herself.*

*And she moved with the light, never wanting to find*
*herself alone in darkness, shivering and cold.*


*She never realised . . . in the fog of her*
*confusion, in her concentration on keeping it*
*all together, in her fight to stay warm . . .*


*She never realised that even alone, she was never cold.*


*Because she was The Sun.*

*Radiant and burning from infinite reserves.*

*Nourishing small creatures and life for millennia*

*Powerful beyond all measure.*

– Ani Aladegbami

# Introduction

# – Devastation

You thought it was one way and it turned out to be another.

Heartbreak hits us so completely, almost violently. It is known and felt in an instant, as if we have been punched. Yet it takes a slow and painful journey of months, sometimes years, to restabilise ourselves and integrate the awful truth of it; the paralysing tiredness that follows is testament to just how much our bodies take the blow. Heartbreak is not just emotional, it's physical, concrete, experienced by our bodies. In heartbreak our bodies temporarily lose their structural and emotional stability and we become vulnerable to everything and everybody around us.

Heartbreak, betrayal, deception, perfidy, treachery, duplicity, faithlessness, abandonment, infidelity, an emotional or physical act constituting a breach of trust; these words represent a violation of safety and a shattering of the core belief central to intimate relationships – trust. Gone is your emotional security, your trust in the appearance of things and the future as you imagined it. The one you trusted has done you great harm, sometimes irreparable harm, and it feels truly awful. It's like being shoved into the Large Hadron Collider and left there indefinitely, or being thrown overboard and – while the waves crash around you and you're struggling to breathe – you look up to your loved one for help, only to realise it was they who chucked you in.

And it's not just the intimate relationship that has been blown apart, but often the entire social and emotional ecosystem that surrounded it and to which you both belonged. The shared friends, the new family, the stories, the history, the favourite haunts – all gone as you find yourself adrift not just from the person you loved but from the network of people and places that glued you together.

Anger, rage, confusion, nausea, sleeplessness, anxiety, sadness, helplessness, dread – replaying and reliving what happened and fantasising about revenge and reconciliation leaves the heartbroken utterly exhausted. It's like being strapped to a knife-thrower's wheel and kept there day after day, going round and round, sharp objects coming thick and fast. It's no wonder that a staggering 67 per cent of betrayed partners meet the criteria for post-traumatic stress disorder (PTSD).[1] There have been various attempts to describe this experience more precisely: post-embitterment disorder[2], post-infidelity stress[3], moral injury.[4]

So grave and heinous is the sin of betrayal, the poet Dante reserved the most awful place in his vision of hell for those who committed it – the ninth and final circle. Next stop, Lucifer himself. In this terrible frozen wilderness, those who commit this 'sin of the heart' are condemned never to feel the warmth of love again. Immersed up to their necks in ice for all time, they lie in grotesque positions, ears frozen off, eyes blinded by icy tears of despair, and with no prospect of reprieve.

Let's leave them there.

Betrayal most often comes to light in a sudden and catastrophic moment of discovery – a graphic sexual message on a phone, a bank statement revealing undisclosed trips, a text message sent to the wrong person. And only then do you see the lies that led up to it, only in retrospect is the web of deceit revealed. Most humans are surprisingly bad lie detectors (something that proficient manipulators exploit), and we tend only to spot their duplicity when it's right in front of our eyes.[5] And being duped feels both painful and humiliating. Added to this is another nasty feeling that lurks in the ashes of the betrayal – contamination. If you discover that your partner has had sex with someone else, you can be left feeling polluted, dirty and contaminated. And, much as an OCD sufferer washes their hands compulsively to rid themselves of germs, the betrayed get locked into an obsessive cycle of rumination in the hope it will rid them of the feelings of humiliation, violation and degradation that accompany the betrayal.[6]

In terms of the magnitude of loss, there is much that heartbreak shares with grief, but with one central difference. Unlike the bereaved, the heartbroken must contend with the feeling of personal rejection, a feeling that cuts right to the place where we are most vulnerable, to the quiet voice inside us all that asks, 'Am I lovable?' And the very person you would usually look to for reassurance is the one who has made you feel that you're not. Heartbreak relegates you to a place of the seemingly unwanted and unloved and with it goes your power. Old pain, sometimes stretching back to childhood, can rear its head in times of rejection, further diminishing your sense of worth and self-esteem. Given this context, it's no wonder that you're spending heroic amounts of mental energy trying to rectify the situation, trying to make it stop by ruminating on all manner of possible scenarios in an attempt to restore a sense of self-worth, punish your heartbreaker, or try to make them love you again.

Love is such a powerful motivator that it has been likened to the rush of taking cocaine. Love releases a flood of dopamine, and the loss of it can leave the heartbroken behaving like drug addicts in search of their next fix.[7] You think you're done with them, but then they throw you a bone (or a crumb) and you're back where you started, grabbing the car keys and driving right over. And the hit is all the stronger if the crumbs are thrown intermittently. The fluctuating dopamine hits of early courtship – *'Do they, don't they love me?'* – are mirrored in the torturous dynamic of heartbreak. One unexpected text message in the dead of night saying they miss you and the dopamine rushes in, compelling you to cling on.

\*\*\*

Heartbreak has long been the subject of songs and novels, but science has largely ignored it in favour of examining the process of falling in love. The lack of guidance from the psychological and scientific community has left the heartbroken to deal with a catastrophic experience of epic proportions with pat phrases like, 'There are plenty more fish in the sea,' or, 'You'll find someone else,' which are completely off-key. When you are betrayed and heartbroken, the last thing on your mind is getting back in the saddle or falling in love again, yet never in human history has it been easier to do just that.

The social revolution of internet dating has created a fast-paced, casual approach to romantic relationships. Take the dating site Ashley Madison[8], whose tagline reads, 'Life is short. Have an affair.' They have an estimated membership of 75.90 million world-wide[9] with nearly 400,000 new accounts opened every month, indicating a mind-blowing amount of infidelity. There is some consensus that infidelity occurs in approximately one quarter of all marriages and monogamous relationships[10] and is the biggest predictor of relationship breakdown and divorce – ahead of incompatibility, falling out of love, addiction and abuse.[11] And the fallout doesn't end there . . .

In 1990s' Japan, doctors in Accident and Emergency noticed anomalies in some patients who were presenting with heart attacks but showing unexpected patterns of injury and recovery. Scans showed an odd shape to the heart, which doctors noted was similar to the shape of pots used to trap octopuses. This led to the condition being named Takotsubo Syndrome (*tako* – octopus; *tsubo* – pot).

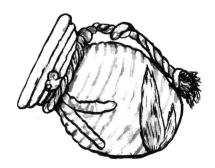

Brought on by stressful and sudden events, such as hearing bad news, financial disaster, unexpected loss, a fierce argument, or even a surprise birthday party, Takotsubo Syndrome (aka Broken Heart Syndrome) has no biological root cause. Its symptoms, however, are indistinguishable from a heart attack:

chest pain, shortness of breath and electrocardiogram abnormalities. Yet, beyond the octopus-pot shape-shift of the heart, there are no other physical signs or arterial obstructions, and unlike the more life-threatening cardiac arrest, recovery is usually quick.[12] Takotsubo Syndrome has since been reported in almost every part of the world. Thousands of people are affected by it every year, and in the UK alone it makes up at least 7 per cent of all heart attack admissions.[13] Furthermore, 90 per cent of those cases occur in women between the ages of fifty-eight and seventy-four.[14] Read that again.

In the West, the leading explanation for this is hormones (feeling hormonal again?) – the depletion of oestrogen during menopause makes women more susceptible to Broken Heart Syndrome as their heart muscles have lost the natural protection against stress that oestrogen provides. But, if this was the whole picture, you'd expect boosting oestrogen through hormone replacement therapy in menopausal women to solve the problem, and yet it doesn't.[15] Similarly, once women reach their mid-seventies and have the least amount of oestrogen – if any – you'd anticipate rates would go up. But again, this is not the case.[16]

In South Korea, the term *haan* describes a feeling of unfairness and helplessness combined with a deep urge to right the wrongs of unresolved injustice. '*Haan*-full' experiences can lead to what the South Koreans term Hwa-Byung – 'fire disease'. Clinically similar to Takotsubo Syndrome, but extending the scope of possible causation, Hwa-Byung is thought to be brought on by injustices and breaches of trust, including infidelity. For the South Koreans, Hwa-Byung is about gender inequality and the suppression of women. Living within narrowly defined roles with little agency and influence over their lives, South Korean women find their anger piling up and up until their hearts give in.[17] Could it be that a lifetime of being in service to others has worn women out? That simply being a woman in this world is enough to break our hearts?

Researchers in Sweden explored more deeply the link between life experience and Broken Heart Syndrome and included men in their study.[18] The interesting thing about their results is that the life experiences of men with Broken Heart Syndrome map almost perfectly onto the women's. Both male and female participants spoke of being 'worn down to the bone' with never ending demands and responsibilities, of being treated unjustly, of not having their own needs met, and, all the while, protecting, helping and worrying about others without sufficient agency to change their situations. Hormones? Maybe. But what the Swedes have found points towards socio-cultural frameworks of power. Far beyond the endocrine system lies the systemic betrayal of those with the least power by those wielding the most.

The truth is that women are still living against a backdrop of marginalisation, disenfranchisement, objectification and subjugation. Embedded within the ecosystems of our relationships, families, social groups and cultures are deeply held values and beliefs. When it is revealed that shared values of equality and justice serve some and not others, we experience not just a personal betrayal but an ideological one. The tendrils of the dominant agenda reach right down into our souls, infusing us with messages that hurt and demean. When we are repeatedly told that we are not enough, that we are worthless, that we lack value, we start to believe it and these messages become internalised. And what's worse is we blame ourselves, as a psychological survival strategy to keep ourselves safe against forces more powerful than us.

Women all over the world are coming alive to themselves, and are fed up with being defined and treated in ways that are diminishing, invalidating and harmful. The #MeToo movement showcased the mighty power of taking a stand together and made public what women have always known – that their lives are not a commodity and that their bodies are not for others.

When women are told it's all because of their hormones; when women are seen to be worthy of less respect and dignity than others; when domestic work done by women all over the world, imperative to their family's survival, is not valued through pay or status; when those in power make legal decisions about women's bodies without consent or adequate consideration; when gender-based violence is tolerated; when women who bring charges of sexual misconduct, assault or abuse are sued for defamation . . .

. . . it is a betrayal.

***

Ruth and I, a coach and a psychologist, have been friends since university, our conversations through the years often turning to our many heartbreaks: bereavement, betrayal, mental illness, rejection, loss of one kind or another and more often than not finding something to laugh at in the face of terrible darkness.

Therapists aren't always that proficient at vulnerability, although our business hinges on being able to help others navigate theirs. In fact, it's not uncommon for therapists to enter the profession precisely to manage and even avoid their own fragilities. Psychological understanding of the kind therapists digest helps create an illusion of structure and understanding around experience and an attendant sense of control. Yet, despite the comforting frameworks, experience and vulnerability always breaks through.

Just as being a doctor doesn't protect you from illness, neither does being a psychologist protect you from pain. I too have succumbed to thoughts of, *I should be over this by now*, and, *No one wants to hear about this anymore.* I can't count how many times I've counselled against this kind of inner talk – holding the flag for loss and heartbreak needing time, and lots of it – and criticised the cultural and societal mores that tell all of us to 'get back up on your feet'.

We have both learnt through personal and professional experience that when we are in pain we need care – intensive care – and that we also need space and time, connection, deep empathy and kindness. This is what you need now, too. To offer you that sense of safety and wraparound care, we've recreated the experience of being on retreat with us, as if you were a guest at The Heartbreak Hotel, searching for answers in the embers of your loss.

Together with your fellow women guests, Nadia, Irene, Eshe, Robyn and Lin, who you'll be meeting soon, we're going to discover what's next for you. Throughout the book we have created scenes, much like a play, where we will be inviting you to step into the space alongside your fellow women and immerse yourself in the experience. Our wish for you, for them, and for all women – is that you rise and shine. And we're going to show you how.

If you're finding it hard to stop scrolling through social media looking at the one they've chosen over you; if you're struggling to find a way to feel differently about your heartbreaker; if your friends have called time on listening to all the drama and if you've tried everything from sound baths to ice baths to hypnosis to drowning your sorrows in wine or sugar; if you take a few steps forward only to be thrown right back into the eye of the storm; if you're feeling as though your soul has been smashed to smithereens and left in pieces on the floor; if you feel helpless and exhausted and depleted and confused and angry and scared of being alone and have forgotten who you are outside of your shattered relationship; if you're railing against the unfairness and injustice and cannot make sense of it all and yet are determined to keep on trying . . .

. . . this book is for you.

# PART I:

# The Present

# Chapter 1:
# Welcome to
# The Heartbreak Hotel

We're glad you're here.

While you're with us, we'd like to invite you to take a break from your responsibilities and let us look after you for a while. What we do is gentle and powerful, and, while you may feel a bit unsure, everything we do has a clear purpose – to get you back together with yourself. It may feel hard at times – we'll be asking you to be with your feelings of heartbreak and to try out new ways of dealing with them – but the act of faith that you are taking now, in being here and placing your trust in us, will be worth it. Take your time, don't hurry yourself. There is no rush.

We want you to feel cocooned in warmth and safety. Heartbreak can be traumatic, so we'd encourage you to wrap yourself up. Have a soft blanket nearby and cosy into it when you feel vulnerable. Create a sense of safety around you: light a candle, diffuse some essential oils and limit interruptions as best you can. Shortly you're going to meet your fellow women. They too have been heartbroken. You will hear echoes of your own experience in theirs, and while you may resonate with some more than others, remember that they are all trying their best in difficult circumstances, just like you. You may get upset as you hear their stories and difficult feelings may surface; this is your empathy and compassion. You need it, we all do, because it is through sharing our vulnerabilities that we connect most deeply to each other and to ourselves.

You may feel exposed at times too, but we want you to know that we will never ask you to do anything that we haven't done ourselves. It is through coming together in this way that we'll begin to reframe what's possible for you, and for all women. Stick with it. You are about to discover what happens when your individual experience is met by the power of the collective.

If you're thinking it all sounds a bit intense and that you're going to be sobbing your way through the experience, rest assured that for every tear shed, there will be joy too. But, we're not going to lie. You're going to get through a lot of tissues. And yet while painful things may come up for you, feelings are like bell curves, they peak and subside, and this is a pattern you will learn to trust as we go along.

Our retreats are alcohol- and technology-free, so we invite you to leave your phone in another room and refrain from the wine while you're with us. Both act as a distraction and numbing influence on your feelings, they offer a way of avoiding them, and avoidance ultimately prolongs suffering. While you're here we want you to have a protected space, where you can be with yourself and each other and where you're not going to be thrown off course by a bottle of wine, or an unsettling message. So just for a while, turn off your phone and give the wine a miss so you can stay with your feelings and not take yourself away from the knowledge and wisdom they contain.

Are you ready?

# Chapter 2:

# Your Story

Before we go on, there is an important task we'd like to invite you to complete. The five women who will be joining you have been asked to do the same:

We would like you to write down the story of what has happened to you, the story of your heartbreak.

Writing down thoughts and feelings has long been used as an outlet and processing device for difficult experiences.[19] Getting it all out and onto the page will create some physical distance so you can start looking *at* your story rather than seeing your experience from *inside* of it.[20] This will help you organise your thoughts and gain clarity over your feelings and experience, creating an opportunity for re-evaluation. When you write down your experience in concrete and explicit terms, your relationship to your heartbreak can shift, positioning you as the narrator of your own experience. The trauma of heartbreak can leave your whole system adrenalised, and writing it down can help process your distress and calm your system.[21]

There is no expectation about how it is written; the length, style, and number of expletives are entirely up to you, and no one else ever needs to read it. We know this can feel hard – you may suddenly remember something vitally important that you have to do right now instead! But remember, getting onto paper what is going round and round in your head is going to give you the control and distance from it that you need.

Imagine a glass of water with a layer of sunken mud at the bottom. Every time you touch the mud, it gets all stirred up and the water turns cloudy. So, you try to leave it alone and avoid it, but walking away just keeps you stuck in the muddy waters. If you want clear water in your glass, you need to get the mud out, and the only way to do this is to stir it up first and then filter it out. Writing down your story is the first step in your journey towards clarity.

If you're not ready to write your story, that's okay, you can wait, and if you don't want to do it at all – ever – that's okay too. But, if you do, we invite you to frame it around the following questions:

What happened to you?

How has it affected you?

What sense have you made of it?

As you write, and as you hear your fellow women's experiences, things may come up for you; this is natural and to be expected. But if you feel yourself becoming distressed or overwhelmed, we'd like to share with you a simple and effective way to help regulate your feelings . . .

## Dropping Anchor

When 'Dropping Anchor', the first thing to do is to accept that the emotional storm is happening.[22] At the same time, expand your awareness of the present moment by noticing two or three things about your surroundings: the smell of clean laundry, the sound of rain on the roof, that the floor beneath your feet is hard or shiny.

Next, push the tips of your fingers together and press your feet into the ground. Take several deep slow breaths . . .

. . . *and accept that the storm is happening.*

Sometimes all we can do is 'Drop Anchor' and hold fast until the storm has passed.

And pass it always does.

As you go through the book, 'Dropping Anchor' is something that you can hold in mind to create a sense of safety and return to whenever you need to. We'll indicate as we go along when we think it might be particularly helpful – and we'll call them 'Dropping Anchor' moments – but for now, while you're taking the time to write your story, you can have a go and practise.

***

As well as metaphors and regulation techniques like this one, we will also be introducing a few meditations along the way. When one is about to come up, we'll let you know and we suggest that you read it through once or twice and then afterwards close your eyes and try to faithfully complete the steps from memory. It doesn't matter if you need to do this a few times to get it right; read it through as many times as you like. After all, there is no rush.

You'll need a pen and paper or journal, so keep these handy while you read on. We invite you to specifically write by hand rather than typing, as this will slow down your thoughts and give you more time to choose your words and connect with your feelings. We'd like you to dig out a photo of your younger self too, somewhere before the age of ten. You don't need to do this right away, but think where one might be and when it's a good time, retrieve it and pop it into your journal or keep it safe for later on.

Okay, let's meet your band of women now and hear what they've been going through.

# Chapter 3:
# Betrayed

**CAST**

NADIA: In her twenties, dark brown hair cropped short and smooth brown skin. Wearing a denim jumpsuit, she has an air of cool detachment. Her hands often disappear into her long-sleeved black T-shirt. She is leaning forward keenly, quietly inquisitive, waiting.

IRENE: A spritely seventy-one-year-old. She has short white hair and wears an oatmeal cardigan with comfy jeans. She is quick to laugh and tease. But there is a hesitancy about her, as if she's not sure if she should be here.

ESHE: In her forties, a senior lecturer in social sciences. She used to go by the name Stella, but since May 2022 has reverted to her birth name. Her wide-set eyes are framed by a mass of neat braids. She wears a loose cotton shirt, and fiddles with the cross on her silver necklace.

ROBYN:    In her sixties. She wears a brightly coloured long dress and matching silver bangles which jangle on her tanned wrists. Her long silver hair is worn loose. She has a small, unopened bottle of gin secreted in her wash bag. She tells herself she won't drink it, but that she needs it near. She's thinking about leaving. Leaving and drinking.

LIN:    In her late thirties, poised and contained, almost painfully polite. She sits up very straight, always close to the edge of her seat, as if quietly striving to occupy the least amount of space. She's worried she won't fit in and seems uncomfortable in her clothes. She admires Ruth's green jumpsuit, even though Ruth tells Lin that her son said she looks like Shrek.

ALICE:    In her late forties, wearing a loose blue dress. She has a quiet confidence and gentleness that puts everyone at ease.

RUTH:    In her mid-forties, wearing a bright green jumpsuit. To be fair, she does look a bit like Shrek. She is smiley and busy and keen to make sure everybody has what they need.

YOU:    Dear reader, yes *you*. Please join us.

# Scene I

## COSY DEN. EVENING

*A cosy den, with two deep blue velvet sofas facing towards a low coffee table. ALICE bends down to light a large candle. A fire crackles in the hearth, an armchair on either side. RUTH pours glasses of water and sets them down, fluffing and plumping cushions as she goes about the room. A low hum reverberates. The sound of footsteps follows and the women enter the room and settle themselves on the sofas. RUTH and ALICE sit in the armchairs on either side of the fire with NADIA to ALICE'S left, followed by IRENE, ESHE, ROBYN, LIN and YOU. Each has brought their story with them, and they all have a blanket at hand.*

RUTH:   [*Standing*] Welcome everybody, it's wonderful to have you here. Get comfy in your seats and let us know if there's anything you need. You may be feeling a bit anxious about your story and that's okay, after all, we've only just met and we are about to do something quite exposing, so it's no wonder we're all feeling a little nervous. It was a big step for you all to write out your stories, and now we're asking you to take another step and read them aloud to a group of almost strangers. We won't be strangers for much longer, that's for sure. So, before we ask each of you to read out your heartbreak story to the group, I'm going to set the intention for us all to be compassionate and kind to one another as we bear witness to each of your painful journeys, by reading aloud a loving-kindness meditation, which we'll do together now. Sound good?

[RUTH *smiles, looks to each woman*]

Okay . . . Here we go . . .

[*Reader: You may want to read this a few times before practising it*]

Take a moment to get settled and turn your attention to the sensations of your heart. We don't often take the time to check in with the state of our heart. Is there tension there? Is there sadness? Relief? Anxiety? Can you feel your heart? Just take a moment to really notice what's there. Not to think about it, but to feel it from the inside out. While you do this, I'd like you to imagine and hold in mind all the women around you who have been heartbroken. Each one is a person who experiences emotions, like you were just noticing inside yourself. Each has been hurt, just like you. Each of them has felt happy at times, just like you. Each has been proud, just like you. Each of these women has felt unworthy or inadequate, just like you. Each of them wants to be happy and content with their life, to feel that their life has meaning, just like you. And each of them has found it hard to achieve these things. Each suffers more than they want to, just like you.

[*Pause*]

See if you can connect with how hard it is to live a human life. Being human is not easy. There may be a sense of heartache or sadness as you contemplate this situation that we all find ourselves in. Here we are, each of us, faced with this situation of how to live a human life. You are now going to silently offer kind wishes to yourself and your fellow women, and as you do, see if you can connect with the sensations and feelings in your heart.

May we all be well.

May we all be joyful.

May we all be safe and at ease.

May we all accept ourselves as we are.

May we all be kind to ourselves.

[*Pause*]

Can you feel right now, in this moment, that you belong to something larger than your own heartbreak? The next time you're in pain, please practise remembering your wish for yourself and your fellow women. Take a moment now to recognise that you have just done something skilful and kind, for yourself and those around you.

It's time now for you to read your stories to each other, and as each of you reads, the rest of us are going to listen with our fullest attention, without judgement or comment. Nadia?

[*The women shift in their seats*]

NADIA: [*Sips water, hands trembling, stands then sits*] I didn't know how to write my story, so I just wrote answers to some of the questions you suggested. But it came out in a different order. Is that okay?

ALICE: However you've written it is exactly right.

NADIA: Okay, here goes ... [*Clears throat, papers quivering*] I met Aanya at a friend's wedding two years ago. I spotted her in the bathroom trying to get a poppy seed from between her teeth, and her lack of self-consciousness made me smile. Later at the bar when I was talking to a friend about how good the food was, Aanya was suddenly standing there telling us how the heat released oils from the curry leaves, which intensified the flavours, and I thought, 'Wow, she's smart.' I soon discovered she was a lab chemist and obsessed with science;

so different from me. I loved listening to her talk about it – amide bonds and oscilloscopes or whatever. And my God, did she love telling me about them. I took her number that night because thankfully the attraction was mutual. I never lived in one place for long as a kid, so I slotted into her world fast; I'm good at that. And six months later we were living together in her flat over-looking the river. Five months after that and she asked me to marry her. Of course I said yes! I was infatuated. My mum ordered silks from Assam for my dress and everyone was so happy for me.

[*Pause*]

Not long after our engagement, Aanya – writing her name still makes me feel so sad – was offered a promo-tion, which meant going to Barcelona for six months. I was happy for her and thought travelling to see her would be fun and it was, for a while. But one day she called me from Spain and said she couldn't go through with the wedding. It came from out of nowhere. I was standing up when I took the call and I sank to the ground when she said that. My knees just gave way. I felt winded, like the life had been punched out of me. I remember gripping the side of the table to steady my-self – it was a wedding gift from my auntie that had been delivered that day and was still in its plastic cover. I remember despite everything that was happening be-ing distracted by the thought of having to return it and explain why. When I finally found my voice, it sounded unfamiliar, as though it belonged to someone else. I was shaking, shivering and talking really fast but I cannot remember much of what I said. My mouth was completely dry. She sounded cold and distant; I didn't recognise her at all. I couldn't understand why she was doing this . . . but she didn't want to talk about it. The call was short, her goodbye so abrupt . . .

[*Pause*]

Then the texting began. I asked her what had happened, implored her to come home, told her she was crazy to throw it all away, pleaded with her to just pick up the phone. I said we'd be okay once we were together again. I was determined that if I carried on as normal, then it wouldn't be happening. She didn't reply to any of my messages.

[*Pause*]

I talked to my cousins and friends. One even offered to call Aanya themselves, but in the end, there was no need. She flew back a week later and the second she set foot inside our flat she told me she'd met someone else. I asked her if she loved her and she said yes, she thought so. I asked her if she'd slept with her and she said she had. I asked her if she still loved me and she said she thought she did, but that she felt trapped. She didn't try to comfort me, even though I was crying and begging her to give us another chance. No matter what question I asked, her answer was the same: it's over. She said it so many times. At one point I fell to my knees, and was holding on to her leg, begging her to reconsider, but she flinched and shook me off like a dog.

[*Lip quivers, teary cheeks,* LIN *passes her tissues*]

[*Pause*]

I can't move on. I keep having the same conversation over and over again with my family and friends and anyone at work who'll listen, and I never get any clearer about anything. They all say if she treated me like that, I'm better off without her, but I just get more upset. I knew she was single-minded and sometimes selfish but I'd always seen this as a good thing. I loved her for it. I just can't believe she dumped me and has left me with all these unanswered questions. It's left me feeling hollowed out. I'm struggling to concentrate at work too, because all I can think about is the other woman. I've since discovered she's a colleague of Aanya's and beautiful in a way that I know I'm not. I can't stop scrolling through her social media; it kills me, but I keep on doing it. I can't sleep. I have nightmares about killing them both, then wake up in a cold sweat and my heart breaks all over again when I realise they are both alive – and probably in bed together. [*Laughs through tears, retreats to the back of the sofa, draws up her knees.* RUTH *wraps a blanket around her. A moment's silence as every-one takes it all in.* ALICE *nods to* IRENE]

IRENE:  Oh right, me now. Gulp. Okay ... Two years after my husband Stan died, my friend Claire persuaded me to join a dating website. It was a week before my seventieth birthday when she came over to help set up my profile. It was a dating site specially for widowers, which in hindsight makes what he did to me even more upsetting. We had a rum and coke, which helped me loosen up a bit, and I even dug out a red lipstick I'd not worn since I was a student nurse in my twenties. We were giggling like a pair of teenagers. I was three rum and cokes down by the time Claire left but do remember admiring my red lips in the mirror and wondering why I'd never worn that lipstick when I was with Stan. I thought it strange I'd kept it for over forty years, and how vivid it was, despite all that time passing. I didn't think anything of the dating site after that – I had mainly done it to please Claire, and it was only when I saw her a week later and she asked me if I'd heard anything that I thought of it again. Soon after that, I got my first message from Daniel. We hit it off immediately. He asked so many questions – I don't remember ever being asked so many – I was flattered by his interest. I opened up to him, about things I'd never even told my husband. Now I just feel like I've betrayed Stan's memory.

[*Pause*]

Daniel called me 'Reeny' and each time he did that, my heart leapt. When we spoke on FaceTime, I'd put on the red lipstick, like a silly teenager. He told me he was working on a rig off Scotland, which Claire checked out to make sure it was true. After a few weeks of talking every day and many messages, he told me his brother had been in a bad accident on the rig and broken both his legs. He said the situation was desperate and that his brother didn't have any money, so I offered to help. Turned out he needed £20,000, which Daniel said he'd pay back as soon as he'd been paid. He even sent me a picture of an invoice, which he said was due to be paid soon, along with a photo of his brother's legs, all mashed up.

[*Pause*]

When I told Claire, she started on me with questions: When were we going to meet up? Why does he keep saying he can't get away? She said they usually have long periods off from the rig, so where was he? I asked Daniel myself, because I was dying to meet him and that's when he told me he was coming to visit in three days. I was so excited. I bought a new outfit and went to the butcher in town to buy haggis – no idea how to cook it, but he'd mentioned he liked it. I couldn't eat a thing in the lead up, I was pacing up and down, in and out of rooms rearranging chairs and putting my lipstick on and then taking it off again. I'm so embarrassed now that I could have been so stupid, like a schoolgirl with a silly crush [*hand on her chest, looking up for reassurance, the women nod*]. But when the doorbell rang and I opened the front door, everything was okay. He was tall, rugged and handsome, with a big smile and neat white teeth. The opposite of my Stan who was ever so stocky and never had much hair. He gave me a huge bear hug, and made me feel at ease right away. It felt so good to have him there after so long being on my own. But I feel like such an idiot now because there were signs. I see them now in neon lights, but not back then. He was always checking his phone, distracted by what kept pinging up.

[*Pause*]

He said it was his brother, but now I know he was having conversations with other women, I don't know how many. In the end, he could only stay the one night, which at the time I thought was romantic as he had travelled overnight from Scotland to get to me. Now I'm wondering if he was ever in Scotland at all. The next morning while we were drinking tea in bed, he started up on his phone again and quickly became upset. More trouble with his brother, who needed money for another round of surgery. I was still so happy from the night before I would have given him the house if he'd asked for it. When I saw the tears in his eyes, what could I do? Of course, I offered to help out. Just before he left, he gave me clear instructions about what to say to the bank when I asked to transfer the money – that it was for renovations on my house so they wouldn't question another large sum. I did exactly as he instructed. But the bank wouldn't do it and kept probing, so I ended up telling them the truth.

[*Pause*]

I called Daniel to let him know what had happened. He got tetchy at first and asked me to repeat exactly what I'd told the bank. I said I couldn't see the harm in being open about his brother, feeling sure they'd understand. He changed then, got so angry and started shouting at me, called me a stupid bitch. I've never had anyone say that to me my whole life. I was stunned, shaking all over, and then I started to cry. He hung up. I didn't know what to do, I was so upset and confused. I'm ashamed to say that I crawled into bed and cried myself to sleep, hoping I'd never wake up. The police got in touch a few days later asking questions and told me they'd uncovered a scam. Turned out Daniel was a fake and part of a much larger criminal operation. I saw red then, and threw that bloody lipstick at the wall. I called him so many times demanding an explanation, but he'd disappeared off the face of the earth. Of course he bloody had.

In the end I had to tell my daughter. I tried to keep it from her, but she could tell something was up. She's the one who found out about this retreat and thought it would do me good. She's so kind to me, sometimes I wonder if I deserve it. My sons are in their thirties and forties and living their own lives and I don't have the heart to tell them. They will think I've been so stupid. And I have. I never should have trusted him. I wanted to spend some time in Australia, visiting my sons and getting to know my grandchildren better. I even entertained the idea of Daniel coming along with me. What a bloody fool I am. I can't believe I'm more heartbroken by a man I only met once and knew online for just a few short months than I was when dear Stan died. I'm sorry. [*Looks up, then buries face in hands, weeping. Room falls silent,* ALL *women looking to* IRENE. ALICE *turns to* ESHE]

ESHE:    [*Clears throat, plays with silver cross on her necklace*] This is so hard . . . We met online and arranged to meet in a local bar where it was immediately apparent he was well known. Looking back I see this held a clue to the sort of man he really is. But I was inexperienced and shy, and, at thirty-five, felt I needed to get on with it. He was intoxicating and I couldn't believe the purity of our connection. It felt so good, it felt right. He was generous in those early days but it turned out he didn't have much money and what little he did have he never held on to for very long. After a while he stopped offering to pay for things, always claiming he was owed money by an unreliable friend. It didn't matter, they were only small things, like cinema tickets or ribs at his favourite restaurant. At the time I paid no attention to the fact none of his friends ever materialised. It was just him and me in a bubble that nothing could pop. I was so happy when he came to my church and met the pastor, and six weeks after our first meeting, he got down on one knee and proposed in front of everyone at the diner. I thought I might die of happiness when he asked, but how quickly it all turned bad. We married within six months, and I became pregnant almost straight away and that's when the cracks started to show. He started staying out late and stopped paying money into our joint account. He lied about his work too, saying he was on a long shift when he was in the bar. He drives a taxi so it wasn't always obvious. When he did come home, though, he was either on at me to do more around the house or to improve my job situation and bring in more money. When I was pregnant with our second child, a head of department role came up which I didn't think I could manage, so I told him I wasn't going to apply for it, and he was so unsupportive. Even though he often came home late, and seemed disinterested in me, I longed for his loving touch, and I did everything I could to try to bring back that warmth, but he left me out in the cold. He was so loving with the children, would laugh and play with them, but switched moods the second I tried to join in. We still had sex, but it became transactional and only ever on his terms. I often wept afterwards, shocked that this intimate beautiful act that had brought us so close together in the beginning could have become so empty. He has this swagger about him and liked to let me know that others were interested and that he could have had anyone, and I believed him. I panicked I'd lose him. I kept thinking I must have caused this change in him; that it was all my fault. That there must be something wrong with me that made him treat me this way. That maybe I was being punished for a crime I had forgotten I'd committed – and I pleaded with God for mercy . . .

[*Pause*]

Straight after the birth of our third child, my father died and I remember my grief was tinged with this intense anxiety about flying back to Johannesburg and leaving him with the other two children, fearful that someone would steal him away from me while I was gone. It was soon after I got back that his phone buzzed while he was in the kitchen and I don't know why I looked, but I did, and then I just couldn't stop. There were all these graphic sexual messages from women with names like Kitten and Cupcake. When he walked back in moments later, I looked up at him in disbelief. He told me of his terrible loneliness, that he didn't feel important and that I'd made him feel small, so he'd sought comfort online – but that was all it had been: online chat sites. He was so vulnerable then, almost like a child, and I felt sorry for him. I forgave him. I held him in my arms and comforted him while he wept, all the time praying that the children would sleep through it. He promised to get help – and that night we made love and his tender touch returned. I was full of hope that things would get better. He said he went to see the pastor to confess and promised to see a counsellor, but he never went, instead using the money I gave him for the sessions to take drugs and have sex in his taxi – and then he gave me an STD. The shame I felt going to the clinic and realising it must have been from him . . . something broke in me that day. Rage rose in me and I chucked all his belongings out of the house and threatened to tell everyone.

[*Pause*]

He has since been back many, many times begging forgiveness. Sometimes he cries. Sometimes he brings me something. Last time he came with a small bunch of yellow freesias that reminded me of home, but they smelled sour, like altar wine gone bad and I threw them out. I am tearful and panicky all the time. I feel like a tent whose middle pole has been snapped in half, and everything is flailing around me untethered. I am left picking up the pieces of our lives and caring for three children while working full time. The worst part is that I still love him, which makes me feel confused and pathetic. How can I love such a man? But the children need their father, and I can't do this on my own.

[ESHE *folds up story, places it in her journal, looks up. Nods shyly, composing herself. After a pause* ALICE *nods to* ROBYN]

ROBYN:   I was diagnosed with multiple sclerosis early last year and within two months my husband of twenty-eight years announced he was leaving me because I was 'boring and crippled'. To begin with I thought it was some kind of sick joke, because he could be a bit like that. But when I realised he was being serious, my next thought was, he's met someone. When I asked him he swore blind that he hadn't and I believed him – I still believe him. I never worried he'd stray because he's never shown any interest in other women. I've never seen him so much as flirt with someone else, because he's too shy for any of that. He told me he wanted to leave because he believes there is a more 'soulful love' out there for him, and for me, and I still don't know what the hell that's supposed to mean.

[*Pause*]

Our daughters don't know yet. They are both away at university and he wants me to tell them. What a coward. I know it will break their hearts and I'm scared that they'll blame me. He should damn well tell them himself. It makes me so mad. I had thought we were a normal, averagely exhausted, happy enough family, but apparently, he was not thinking the same way and was not happy at all. He now says that he never felt close to me, that we never had a deep connection. He told me that I was no fun and made him miserable, but that's just not true! I'm not sure of anything anymore. By the way, all these precious insights are coming to me via text message from France where he is camping out in the house we've spent the last decade renovating – our retirement project. He's probably installing the mosaic bathroom tiles we found on a trip to Santorini – I hate them now. Anyway, to say I am heartbroken would be an understatement. The horror of it all just keeps coming over me in waves. I thought we were okay. Our sex life wasn't great, I'll admit that. But I was wiped out a lot and going through the menopause so I put it down to that. Plus, he'd never had much of a sex drive himself, so it didn't occur to me that this might be a big deal. It feels as though at the first hint of sickness, everything we'd built together came tumbling down. I am slowly realising that I have been the only adult in our marriage. I had three children to look after, one of them being my husband.

[*Pause*]

He is intent on a divorce but he wants me to organise it all for him! I am left alone in the house we shared for more than thirty years. Our marriage is everywhere and all around me. I am afraid of the financial implications of all this for my future, but more than that, I'm terrified of being alone. I am too old to start again, and I have no idea who I am anymore. I cannot make sense of it. I've been going through old photo albums searching for clues to explain his sudden disappearance. We weren't miserable, we barely even argued. I can only think that since his work has slowed down and he's spent more time at home that he's having some sort of crisis. I'm devastated that it's come to this. That's it. [ROBYN *looks up, then casts eyes down*]

LIN:    [*Twiddling strands of hair between fingers, eyes flit between* ALICE *and* RUTH] Okay, here goes . . . Every time I put my key into the lock, I hold my breath. Sometimes, it's silent inside and I'll call out his name to check if he's there. Often he doesn't answer, so I assume he's out, but then I find him lying in the bath, which makes me jump, and then he sneers at me for getting spooked. Or he'll be lying on the bed fully clothed with his arms across his chest, staring at the ceiling waiting to catch me out. I am very careful about what I say to him on these occasions, if anything. But when I open the door to the smell of his delicious cooking, I'll feel hopeful again. This is now so infrequent that I'm starting to wonder if it ever actually happened. It's got to the point where the smallest thing can set him off, like not hanging my keys on the correct hook. I never thought I'd miss the days when he was sulking in the bath or lying on the bed, but I do sometimes. Anything is better than his contempt.

*[Pause]*

It wasn't always like this. In the beginning, we were happily exhausted medics working in different parts of the hospital. I was a junior house officer in Radiology up on the third floor, and he was a consultant anaesthesiologist working in the Intensive Care Unit, raising people from the dead – that's how my mother put it. I still fantasise about those early days when he couldn't keep his eyes off me. We were never apart; we'd spend hours wandering through the botanical gardens holding hands and talking. I loved how he looked after himself and treasured all his belongings. Perhaps I should have thought that was odd, but at the time I thought it was a sign of his good character – that he took such good care of them meant he'd take good care of me.

*[Pause]*

We used to mark off our shifts on the kitchen calendar and coordinate our days off so we could spend them together. But not anymore. Everything changed when he moved hospitals last year. He became possessive of my time and suspicious of what I was doing with it, and if I ran over my shift, he'd quiz me at length and always find fault with my answers. I dreaded my pager sounding with last-minute emergencies, afraid of provoking him, but all I have to cling to now is my work, and I am so grateful for it. On the nights when he isn't at home,

I've trained myself to enjoy the fact that I have the place to myself and can leave my keys wherever I want.

[*Pause*]

When I'm shattered, he plays music to torment me or sings loudly in the shower just as I'm going to sleep. And whenever we are off work at the same time, he leaves the apartment, overnight bag in hand, almost the minute I'm home, no goodbye and no telling me where he's going. I know he doesn't visit his parents or sister. I have no idea where he goes or who he is with. He doesn't answer his phone or respond to my text messages, so I've stopped sending them. When I get home and he's back from one of these outings, I'll find him asleep smelling of someone else. He likes to keep me guessing and enjoys baiting me, but if I dare to question him too much, he flies off the handle. When I get upset, he shouts that I'm imagining things, that I've made it all up, that I am a nightmare to live with. The rest of the time there is this deafening silence, the atmosphere so harsh and devastating, I feel like I could die. I found a scarf that didn't belong to me and confronted him about it. He flung it in my face and said I was talking rubbish, that it was the scarf he'd bought me last Christmas. He had bought me a scarf, but it was not bright pink or made of silk like this one. He sounded so sure about it and was so angry at me for accusing him, that in the moment I thought he might be right and perhaps I had made a mistake. Two weeks ago, I tried to tell him I wanted him to leave my apartment, but he laughed in my face and told me he wasn't going anywhere. He said nobody else would ever want me, that I'd be on my own forever. I was stunned that he could just dismiss me like that and carry on scrolling through his phone as if I hadn't said anything at all. I felt I was worth less than nothing to him [*pauses, a few deep breaths, looks up, smiles at* ALL].

I was desperate and had no one to turn to, so I plucked up the courage to call my mother. I'd barely got going when she told me how lucky I am to have attracted the attention of a consultant anaesthesiologist and that whatever sins he has committed I must forgive. I should have known better than to hope for anything from her [*voice trails off*]. I hate myself for being so weak [*raises eyes, tears fall*].

ALICE:   Reader, are you ready to share your story with us?

[*Invites the group to check in with how they are feeling in their bodies and encourages them to bring to mind 'Dropping Anchor,' if they need to.*]

# Chapter 4:
# Rumination – The Trap

*Did they use sex toys? Did they use one of these? Tap tap tap. Which ones? How long ago? Did they watch porn together? What kind? How recently? Did she tell her about me? When? Where? How? Is that another lie? Are they together now? Scroll scroll scroll. Instagram, WhatsApp, Facebook, head on fire, pulse racing, burn burn burn. Hold head, squeeze eyes, rock rock rock. How could she? Why why why? I don't understand. I'm going to be sick, I'm going to be sick, flick flick flick.*

Nadia went over and over again in her mind what might be on her fiancé's phone. She imagined into existence all sorts of unspeakable sexual acts, endless mental images of her fiancé and her lover together, causing her acute pain. It was a compulsion, a form of self-harm she felt powerless to stop.

She spent many evenings with her cousin after she discovered her fiancé's infidelity. They'd drink wine late into the night, poring over texts and photos. Nadia would tell her cousin again and again about the awfulness and injustice of it all. Her cousin listened, wondering if it even mattered to Nadia that she was there. Because it wasn't a conversation; it was her internal dialogue externalised, her attempt to get clarity on an unbearable situation that made no sense. It was an attempt to try to reach some kind of resolution so she could move forward. And she was angry. Very, very angry. Stuck in an endless loop of questions, desperate for answers that never came, Nadia was in terrible pain and her cousin felt helpless. Any attempt to encourage her to stay with one point and examine it would be quickly swatted away. She didn't want to hear it. So, on and on she went. Round and round and round. And in the dead of night her quest for answers would take on a quieter and more troubling undertone that whispered, *There's something wrong with you.*

The foundations of rumination go deep, beyond the event itself to the very heart of our sense of self and the world around us. The existential imperative to understand our world and our lives is cloaked with another human need – to feel loved.

Nadia needed her anger and her quest for answers because it kept her from the painful feeling of no longer being loved. Her rumination seemed to be the only power she had left, the only control she could exert over her freefall. And, in fact, there *was* a purpose to Nadia's rumination. It was a necessary protection her mind and body generated to shield her from the unbearable loss, bewilderment and rejection that lay beneath her frenetic search for resolution.

\*\*\*

Heartbreak creates an unbearable dissonance, a catastrophic split between how we thought things were and how they now appear to be. And the rumination is an attempt to restore equilibrium and create consonance once again. As meaning-making beings, we like to create organised frameworks and systems to inhabit in order to feel safe. If how we previously understood relationships conflicts with where we now find ourselves, we become intensely confused and anxious – it makes no sense.[23] Under the extreme distress and anger of rejection, our meaning-making machinery goes into overdrive, desperately trying to restore alignment.

Rumination is natural and inevitable in the aftermath of betrayal, and the fact that you do it is a symptom of your intelligence. You are trying to figure things out and gain a sense of control, to reconcile what has happened, and make meaning from the wreckage. You are trying to put it all back together somehow, to repair it and to feel hopeful again. But then you can't sleep for thinking how it all came to pass, why it happened, how you didn't deserve it and how alone and tired you are . . . how unjust the world is. So, you try to think even harder to put it all to rights, and the vicious loop continues.

And the body takes the blow too. The headaches, accelerating heart rate, shaking and nausea are all indicative of a body in high tension and stress. It's in the sleeplessness and frantic worry, the lack of concentration, the poleaxing exhaustion as you rip along at breakneck speed on the rumination roller coaster you never wanted to board but somehow now cannot get off.

Rumination taunts and torments you like a jailer, keeping you awake and threatening you with a life sentence while the person who has the answers is either long gone or disinterested in your need for them. It's torturous.

Your mind focuses in on the hostile event and gets stuck like an old record, repeating the same cycle, rarely giving you a conclusive or satisfactory answer . . . and it's a costly business. It's like a repeated withdrawal of funds from your emotional tank and, before you know it, you're all out, in the red, and being charged interest for the overdraft.

So powerful is it, that the rumination is almost impossible to contain and ends up spilling out into all your conversations and relationships. The heartbroken frequently enlist the help of friends to go over their betrayal in increasingly indignant circles of 'co-rumination'.[24] And the bigger the badder: As more and more friends are unwittingly enlisted into the rumination, it becomes a collective project. Yet this collective rumination, far from alleviating the pain, actually intensifies and accentuates your suffering by keeping you locked into the endless quest.[25] 'Collective rumination', as it's known, can maintain anger not just for months or years, but through generations.[26]

As well as fuelling your anger and increasing the stress in your body, rumination can reduce self-control.[27] In a ruminative frame of mind, you're left vulnerable to actions that you might later regret. Ever pressed send on a vitriolic text message you immediately wished you could retrieve? Driven over to your heartbreaker's house and banged on the door? Followed their new lover online or in person? Taken up smoking? Drunk excessive amounts of alcohol? Far from giving you control, rumination and its attendant stress can actually disable the stop button. And you can't just tell yourself to stop. What you resist persists and telling yourself to stop only serves to keep the thoughts coming – often faster and more intensely. If we were to ask you *not* to think about a pink elephant for the next minute, could you do it? Have a go. It's a frustrating paradox: you can't tell your rumination to stop because that only intensifies it, and yet it's only when your rumination stops that you can get out of the cycle and move forward.

There is another way . . .

Letting go is the act of deciding not to struggle anymore with what has happened. It's not letting go of a person; your heart and mind will forever be populated by the people you have loved, even the ones who have hurt you. It is letting go of the struggle – day after day.

## The Tiger Cub

Imagine you wake up one morning and just outside your front door is an adorable tiger kitten, meowing.[28] Of course, you bring the cuddly little thing inside to keep it as a pet. After playing with it for a while, you notice it is still meowing, nonstop, and you realise it must be hungry. You feed it a bit of minced meat, knowing that's what tigers like to eat. You do this every day, and every day your pet tiger grows a bit bigger. Over the course of two years, your tiger's daily meals change from hamburger scraps to prime rib, to entire sides of beef. Soon your little pet no longer meows when hungry. Instead, it growls ferociously at you whenever it thinks it is mealtime. Your cute little pet has turned into an uncontrollable savage beast that will tear you apart if it doesn't get what it wants.

Every time you feed it, you help your tiger grow a little bit larger and a little bit stronger. Feeding it in this manner seems like the prudent thing to do; either you feed it whatever it wants, or it will eat you up. Yet every time you feed it, you enable the tiger to grow stronger and more intimidating . . . until the tiger controls you.

Your pain is the tiger, and your rumination is the food. The solution that rumination promised to be turns out to be the problem – now on steroids – that it was supposed to solve.

## The Chinese Finger Trap

Struggling won't set you free.[29] When you are trapped in an experience, feeling as though you're drowning and are going to be swallowed up by it, your instinct is to try to escape. Everything in you screams, 'Get out! Find a way out! I can't bear it! Struggle more! Pull harder!' This is a completely natural survival strategy, and a useful one at times because it's your instinct talking. But there are some situations you can't escape in this way. Sometimes, struggling creates more of a noose than the rope itself. Think of quicksand, where the frantic movements of your body shift the sand so it sucks you further under. The way out – counterintuitive though it may seem – is to stay still, spread your body out, and float on the sand until it releases its grip so you can call for help or roll over to safety. We don't recommend you experiment with quicksand, but we do have something else to help you absorb the idea in a less gritty way – the Chinese Finger Trap.

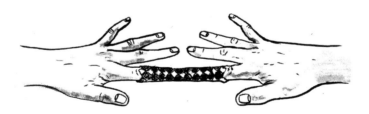

This is a woven bamboo tube, not more than a few inches long, just wide enough for you to fit your index fingers inside. But once you've placed them inside, if you try to pull them out again, the weave of the bamboo constricts and the grip on your fingers tightens. The harder you struggle to get them out, the tighter the grip becomes. Maintain the force of the pull and you stay right where you are, trapped. If, on the other hand, you relax your pull and let your fingers just exist inside the trap with no tension at all, the weave of the bamboo slackens and expands, and you find there is ample room to remove your fingers and make good your escape.

The more you try to think your way out of the pain, the tighter the grip it has on you. Nothing is going to take the pain away, and we know it hurts like hell, but in noticing when you're back in the struggle again, and choosing instead to let go, is how you'll begin to reframe your relationship to it. So, try to remember the Chinese Finger Trap – buy one if you like! – and use it as a reminder of how to let go.

# Chapter 5:

# Give your Ex the Finger

**Scene II**

**COSY DEN. LATER THAT EVENING**

> *Fire crackles, the sound of footsteps as the women re-enter the room and settle themselves back down. NADIA wraps a blanket around her shoulders, sinking back into the sofa corner. IRENE sits at the other end, placing a folded square of blanket on her lap, pats it down. ROBYN on the opposite sofa, facing IRENE, is sipping water. LIN sits close to the edge of the sofa and shivers. ESHE moves to LIN, takes a blanket from the sofa arm, drapes it around her, giving LIN'S shoulders a squeeze, before settling into her seat. ESHE sits cross-legged, leans in, fiddling with her necklace.*

RUTH: We're going to have some fun now and do a short exercise together.[30] It's lighthearted, but the purpose is deep

– to reduce the power of your heartbreaker and all the nasty things they've said to you. We're going to do this by externalising and then diffusing those criticisms, so they no longer feel as though they are part of who you are. Are you ready? Let the diffusion begin!

First of all, I want you to picture your heartbreaker: really see them in your mind's eye. I want you to imagine a time when they were really critical and harsh. It might be an isolated incident, it might be a barrage of criticism, it doesn't matter, just bring it to mind and really hear them saying those nasty things to you. Now I want you to tune into their tone of voice while they're saying it – is it loud, harsh, shouty? Really hear it. Have you got it? Okay. Now I want you to change the voice and make it really high-pitched and squeaky, like a cartoon character, and have them say the mean things in this new silly voice instead. Have you got it? Okay, great . . . Now extend your forearm straight in front of you as far as it will go, palm upturned. It doesn't matter which arm you use, whichever feels most comfortable. Curl up your fingers into your palm and make a fist. . . now raise the middle finger. Okay . . . take the image in mind of your heartbreaker and transport this image out from your mind and float it all the way down your arm and onto the tip of your middle finger, and as you do so, shrink them down to the size of a thimble so they fit on the tip. Are they there? Can you see them, all tiny over there on the end of your finger? Now that you have them over there, barely bigger than a peanut, can you also imagine just how squeaky and high-pitched their voice has become, now that they are so very small?

[ALL *intently looking at middle finger,* ROBYN *drops left arm, raises right*]

Now that they're way over there on the tip of your finger speaking in that silly, tiny squeaky voice, I want you to hear them saying all those nasty things again: the excuses, lies, false promises and criticisms, but whenever they speak, whatever it is they say, make sure they are saying it in their tiny squeaky voice. And now if you want to, you can give them a new name, something really silly. There's no judgement, just whatever comes to mind. Nadia?

NADIA:  [*Nervous smile playing on lips*] I'm calling her Frosty and she's saying, 'You'd better join the gym or you'll end up as fat as your mum.'

[*Intake of breath from* ALL, ROBYN *tuts disapproval*]

RUTH:   Is there anything you'd like to say to her now?

NADIA:  [*Frowning, bullish*] You are wrong, I'm nothing like my mother. You think you'll be happier with *her,* but you won't be, and – by the way – you're the one who needs the fucking gym [*sits*].

IRENE:    [*Confidently rising, unleashing middle finger as if spring-loaded*] You're a stupid bitch. [*Pause*] You're a stupid bitch [*pitch of voice rising*]. You're a stupid bitch.

[NADIA *and* ROBYN *gasp*]

RUTH:    What is his new name, Irene?

IRENE:    Lucifer.

RUTH:    Is there anything you'd like to say to him now?

IRENE:    Go to hell.

[ALL *laugh,* IRENE *bows and sits, flushed*]

RUTH:    Eshe?

ESHE:    [*Face scrunched, fiddling with silver cross, hesitant*] I can't do it. I don't want to mock him like that.

RUTH:    That's okay, Eshe. This is just a technique, and one of many we'll be using that can help reduce their hold over you. We can come back to it later if you like?
         [*Long pause,* ESHE *twists cross, room falls silent*]

ESHE:    I think I can do the name bit ... It's ... Ballsack [*relieved*].

RUTH:      [*Smiling*] That's a big step, Eshe, well done. Robyn?

ROBYN:     [*Glaring hard at tip of finger, voice like she's inhaled helium*] I'm leaving you for someone fun who's not riddled with disease.
           [ALL *silent, unsure whether to laugh or cry*]

RUTH:      And his name?

ROBYN:     [*With conviction*] Voldemort.

RUTH:      Is there anything you'd like to say to him now?

ROBYN:     Yeah there is. Fuck you and your 'soulful love' bullshit [ALL *laugh in relief*].

LIN:       [*Rising to her feet without prompt, arm extended with purpose*] You're mad, bad and sad.

RUTH:      And his name?

LIN:       Dickdust.

RUTH:      What would you like to say to him now?

LIN:       [*Nodding*] You're not worthy of my love.

           [ESHE *looks to* RUTH *and stands*]

RUTH:   When you're ready, Eshe.

ESHE:   [*Slowly, deliberately extending finger*] What's wrong with you? This place is a pigsty. I'm not putting up with it anymore.

[*Sharp intake from* ALL]

RUTH:   [*Gently*] Is there anything you'd like to say to him now?

ESHE:   You're a liar and a cheat. You're no good!

[ALL *clap*]

RUTH:   Reader, are YOU ready to have a go?

[*Pause*]

Okay, great. So now every time the voice of your heartbreaker comes to mind, you know what to do . . . give them the finger.

# Chapter 6:

# Radical Acceptance – The Art of Letting Go

Soon enough you will find yourself back in the intrusive rumination cycle, trying once again to work it all out, plotting heinous punishments for your ex – bringing them down, destroying them. Don't judge yourself for doing this. Take a deep breath and read these words aloud:

> Things are not as I want them to be,
> Nor as they should be.
> They are as they are.

This is radical acceptance[31] and it is a choice we can make both in the moment, and as an ongoing process. It's an acceptance of what is *as it is*. This is not the same as approval or resignation, and it's not forgiveness or surrender. Radical acceptance is never a passive act. It's a downing of tools, a conscious, active decision not to struggle anymore. What has happened has happened and no amount of struggling with it will change that.

And, let's face it, radical times need radical solutions.

*Radical* because it means going all the way; it's a total acceptance of the fundamental and complete nature of the situation, and all that has led to it, without exceptions or caveats. *Radical* because the consequences are far reaching, and the change generated is felt at the deepest level. *Radical* because radicals advocate for change and are often revolutionary.

In Hindi, *radical* means 'fiery' and 'fierce'. We like the juxtaposition of fiery and fierce with acceptance because it changes its energy into something altogether more powerful and alive. It bestows upon *radical* a seismic quality that it deserves.

We don't usually think of acceptance as being a precursor to change, but it is. It is the intentional act of accepting what has already happened so that you can clear a space to think about what's next.

Betrayal creates a dialectical tension where two things exist together even though they seem to contradict one another: I love them and hate them; I want to stay and go; I want to kill them and kiss them; they are my safe and my dangerous person. Trying to resolve this tension leads to deadlock. But radically accepting the natural presence of this unavoidable tension releases you from the pressure to eliminate it.

Acknowledge and accept that the unjustified, unfair, monstrous thing has happened, and that however much you try to think your way out of it, it is now in your life. We are inviting you to incorporate it into your life rather than keep fighting against it. In accepting this, you are also accepting all the things that happened before this moment, including your part in them. Nothing in the past can be changed, and it has all led to this moment, which also can't be changed.

Let this sink in.

***

Imagine you have an important meeting at 9 a.m. and the bus you're on is stuck in traffic, and it looks like you're going to be late. You have two choices. You can fight it and be angry, worry about the consequences of your lateness, stress about the fact that you're stressed . . . enter into yet another round of the rumination battle to figure it out, restore justice, punish the perpetrator (or the bus driver). Or . . . you can radically accept it, and as the bus inches forward, distract your mind and turn up the tunes. The bus will be late either way, but only one route offers a path to peace.

Radical acceptance doesn't change the facts, it changes the outcome. Your heart rate goes down, your body releases its tension, your breathing slows and you can begin to restore balance to mind and body. In *this* state of being we are powerful – in spite of what has happened.

How much energy have you spent resisting it, agonising over the 'what ifs?', trying to figure out *'why me?'*

That very question is predicated on the idea that the world is fair and just. That bad things don't happen to good people, that good things shouldn't happen to bad people. This is not how it is. Why you? Why *not* you?

We all fall into this trap – it's a human way of trying to make sense of a complex world. But unfortunately, bad things can happen to anyone. If you radically accept the radically unfair, even though it may make no sense, you will set yourself free. Radical acceptance represents the start of a new way of being.

Things are not as I want them to be,
Nor as they should be.
They are as they are.

Learn it by heart and have it on repeat.

## The Troll and the Hole

Imagine you're in a game of tug-of-war with your heartbreak.[32] You hold one end of the rope and on the other end is a scary looking troll who represents all your unwanted thoughts and feelings. Between you and the troll is a huge black hole and you sense that it contains something awful. Maybe it's a crocodile? Maybe it's a snake? Or maybe it's an endless spinning into existential nothingness?

So, you keep fighting, holding on to that rope, not giving in an inch, terrified of both the hole and the troll. Your hand is sore, you're very thirsty, possibly in need of a snack, and you're not sure how much longer you can keep going.

But there is a way out of this exhausting and frightening situation, which you haven't yet turned your mind to, so hard have you been trying to win.

Let go of the rope.

Because when you let go, no one goes near the hole. Instead, you fall backwards, dust yourself off and walk away to get on with something else. All the energy you have been expending in the tug-of-war is freed up.

You win by letting go of the struggle. And when you do, your thoughts are released, just as you are. The resolution lies in doing the opposite of what you might expect.

It's also important to manage expectations. Even though you might have promised yourself to practise radical acceptance, you will forget, or find yourself not wanting to do it, and you will inevitably fall into the trap of trying to figure it all out again.

That's okay. Gently notice when this happens and remind yourself that you are probably trying to resolve the dialectic tension of betrayal – and feel very clever in the process.

If you need more convincing, try half an hour of intense struggle, ruminate your heart out, and then half an hour of radical acceptance. Which felt better?

By now you will have noticed that most of the exercises you have been introduced to centre around going with and letting go. This may not be how you are used to operating. If you are feeling uncomfortable with the idea, remember 'Dropping Anchor' – this will help to build a sense of safety as you move forward. Know that you can do this whenever you wish, to help your body and spirit relax.

In choosing to radically accept what has happened, you cease to give your energy to someone who has broken your heart and can use it instead to re-ignite the flame within. It allows you to be more powerful and freer than you ever imagined. You are an enormous force for good and an agent for change who can define yourself according to what is important – as *you* see it.

# Chapter 7:

# The Vow of Silence

Your brain is trying to process what has happened and why. But as we now know, rumination offers only false promises; it's a ghoulish masquerade. What your rumination is really doing is helping you avoid the real and awful undercurrent: that you have been heartbroken. Of course, you would rather avoid that, but remember, the rumination is your jailer, not your friend. The journey to freedom can only begin once you stop struggling with what has happened. We know this is hard, and so to help you, we're inviting you now to take a vow of silence. It is a moratorium on talking about your heartbreaker for the time that you are with us, and acts as a rumination container. It also represents the moment we turn away from them and keep the focus firmly on you. The reality is that your heartbreaker is irrelevant to your onwards journey. You will want to speak of them, and you can, but when you do, reminding yourself that you took this vow will present you again with a choice of where to redirect your energy – back towards the heartbreaker or . . . onwards – towards yourself.

You will most likely need to keep on taking this vow, and that's okay. It's not about nailing it from the get-go, but about a whole-hearted commitment to giving it your best shot – and to keep on trying.

Say after me . . .

'From this moment forward, I vow not to talk about my heart-breaker. I will keep the focus firmly on myself so that I may flourish and grow.'

You will have feelings about this. Notice them, see if you can name them. Feelings have a reliable arc: they reach a moment of highest intensity, inevitably peak and then subside – it may *feel* overwhelming, but it won't actually overwhelm you. Go *with* the feeling rather than fighting against it.

Riptides are pockets in the sea where the current is going in the opposite direction to what you'd expect. You might swim out from the beach, then turn around and try to swim back only to find that the tide is now pulling you further out. You try to swim harder and faster, but you're going nowhere and the panic rises. You must get back to the shore! But if you keep swimming against the tide, you will continue to get nowhere. The only thing that happens is you exhaust yourself.

What you need to do is take a leap of faith and let the tide take you further out to sea. Once you are released from the rip-tide you can swim around it safely and then head back to shore.

Struggling against your feelings means living in fear that they will overwhelm you if you let them come, and this fear alone will intensify their potency and leave you with double trouble – the feeling *and* the fear of the feeling.

It's only through letting your feelings be that you discover this.

It's natural to fear that your feelings will drown you, but they won't, not if you go with them. We are conditioned to escape danger and negative states through suppressing, denying, numbing, getting away from and scrambling for solutions. And all of these strategies are needed, sometimes. But if you let yourself feel, and yes you will experience the intensity of your feelings, you will also learn that it won't go on forever – it will always subside. Problems are created when you consistently shut your feelings off, guard against them, and live with anxiety about when they might come back. If you act to get rid of them before the peak – by drinking, distracting or solving – you don't ever get to the other side.

The desire to avoid painful feelings through distraction and rumination is strong and difficult to resist, which is why you have taken this vow until you have finished reading this book. From now on, if you need to mention them at all, you can either use the name you created for them when you gave them the finger or refer to them as your 'unmentionable'.

# PART II:

# The Past

# Chapter 8:

# Bonding Blueprints

Almost without exception, humans have a deep and primal need to feel connected to the people, places and systems that surround them. Buried deep within our genomes[33], the need to feel accepted, respected, included and loved is as fundamental as the need for food and shelter. Siblings, parents, friends, teachers, the wider community, they all have a bearing on our sense of security and belonging and ultimately how we feel about ourselves – and like a golden thread stretching back to our earliest days, these first relationships create the bonding blueprints for all subsequent ones.

What was your early nest like? Was it soft and cosy like a hummingbird's, or sturdy and large like an eagle's? Who was in it with you? Was there a big noisy brood, or just you? What were the sounds, smells, atmosphere? Was life predictable, did you know what to expect, or was it chaotic and scary? What was the ecosystem around it like – the social and cultural messages that influenced how you felt about the world? Take a moment to think about or write down your thoughts.

Your experience in the early nest gave rise to fledgling beliefs about how the world works, acting like an internal map navigating all your relationships and experiences to come. Your brain's neural pathways are at their most active around the age of two[34], firing on all cylinders, reorganising and adapting themselves in response to your experiences. Childhood is a very busy time of meaning-making and pattern formation; it is when we start to decide things about ourselves, others and the world. And these nascent understandings are powerful and persistent. Childhood is a time when you are figuring out not just whether other people can be trusted, but also your sense of your own worth.

While much of your internal map has helped guide you into becoming the person you are today, some of the information contained in those early fledgling beliefs may be clipping your wings and steering you off course. Because – adaptable as we are as children – we don't yet have a full arsenal of understanding to comprehend the complexities of adult relationships and the world around us.

You may not wish to go back and look at your childhood. We have this in mind and will go gently.

Heartbreak represents an interpersonal rupture, one that can activate our past knowledge and experience of others and ourselves. When the bond is broken, we try to mitigate the distress and our internal map is triggered into action. Our early bonding blueprints are activated, and it's worth taking a closer look at these because they can influence not just how much distress we feel when we are heartbroken, but also our perceptions of ourselves and our partners.

Our intention is to use the full power of your adult mind to take another look at what was happening in your early nest, to understand how you made sense of it back then, and to shine an empathic and understanding adult perspective on it, so you have everything you need to ride out this storm with confidence. Feelings may come up as we go along: remember they are important. You need them.

*** 

Picture this . . .

Back in the 1960s, American psychologist Harry Harlow conducted a series of shockingly cruel experiments on a group of baby rhesus macaque monkeys.[35] The baby monkeys were removed from their mothers shortly after birth and put alone in a cage with two inanimate 'mother' substitutes, one covered with soft, cosy cloth, and the other made of bare wire, but with a bottle of milk attached.

Harlow was interested to see which need the monkeys prioritised: the need for food or the need for comfort. The babies went straight to the cosy look-a-like, even when they were hungry.

As if this set-up wasn't brutal enough, the researchers then removed the cuddly 'mother' and replaced her with a teddy bear that made loud scary noises. And even though the wiry 'mother' was present, the terrified baby macaques didn't reach for her, instead they screamed and crouched in fear, covering their heads, sucking their thumbs and rocking back and forth.

Harlow's experiments demonstrated that without comfort, baby macaques couldn't regulate their fear. The monkeys who grew up with these 'fake' mothers found it hard to know how to cope. They were timid and struggled to stand up for themselves, were less curious, and had more difficulty mating and making friends – in short, they felt unsafe. And they did what they needed to do to feel safer: they became submissive and hid themselves away in order not to be harmed. And it worked for a while, until they got bigger and were put in more complex environments where they doubled down on their original strategy of self-subordination. But rather than making them safe, the unintended consequences of their strategy was that they were vulnerable to being picked on. Not because there was anything wrong with them, but because what had happened to them at the hands of Harlow meant that they had learnt to respond to unsafe situations by being unthreatening. And far from making them safer, it made them more vulnerable to those who might take advantage.

These unethical experiments marked a turning point away from the Victorian idea that to comfort children was to spoil them and that their emotional needs were irrelevant, paving the way for Attachment Theory[36], the idea that infants need reassurance and comfort from a responsive caregiver to feel safe, and the extent to which they receive it forms the bonding blueprint by which they navigate all future relationships – long after they've flown the nest.

Early bonding blueprints act as an emotional mapping system, giving us coordinates to navigate the relational world with a sense of predictability and safety. If we didn't have them, we'd be very much at sea. It is only once we spread our wings, leave the nest and take to the open skies that these beliefs and strategies are put to the test.

If you were lucky enough to have had an early nest where your caregivers were responsive to your younger self's needs, you will have felt more or less secure and developed a bonding blueprint that reflects this. Your emotional regulation system will be well developed, and you can use it to navigate choppy waters. Growing up with a warm and caring atmosphere around you and having your needs met and your feelings valued will have given you a sense of safety growing up. You will feel settled and calm in relationships, and intimacy and commitment will feel good. You are likely to have a strong and solid sense of yourself, can negotiate conflict well, are emotionally stable, and can manage the ups and downs of relationships with relative ease. Power struggles are rare and you are generally supportive and empathic and able to ask for help when you need it. You tend towards feeling sunny and safe. You are securely attached, the **Safe Harbours**.[37]

If your early caregivers were unresponsive to your emotional – and perhaps physical – needs, you will have felt insecure and unsafe in your early nest. You will have tried out all your available emotional responses, but quickly learnt that in the unsafe environment – just like the monkeys – some responses kept you safer than others. And we all hold on very tightly to what keeps us feeling safe, so these strategies can be highly resistant to change, even when different strategies might work better. For some, this might mean avoiding getting too close – the **Lone Rangers**[38]; for others, it might be trying to stay very close – the **Close Rangers**.[39] Some of you might not be sure whether it's safer to be close or distant – the **Roller Rangers**.[40]

Let's take a closer look . . .

**Lone Rangers**. If you are self-reliant and independent in relationships and feel uncomfortable if the emotional temperature gets too hot, you may be a Lone Ranger. While able to be warm and loving, Lone Rangers can find the challenges of intimacy threatening. Emotional closeness reveals their deeper feelings and when they are under pressure it can leave them wanting to flee – their feelings can't be trusted so it is better to keep away. Conflict can feel threatening too, and Lone Rangers tend to be evasive and distant to guard against feeling unsafe. Their early nests were characterised by a lack of responsiveness from their caregivers, *or* over-controlling, overbearing ones. Ultimately, Lone Rangers did what they needed to do to keep safe – developed the protective strategies of self-sufficiency and independence. If emotional proximity feels overwhelming and you hate the idea of being tied down, this could be you. A classic Lone Ranger might respond to the question, 'How come you've never settled down?' with, 'I just haven't met the right person.' In this way, Lone Rangers centre the problem outside of themselves and avoid exposing their own vulnerability. Often unaware of their own distress, they tend to suppress their attachment needs and seek independence to regulate their experience. Their blueprint mapping system looks a bit like this:

*If* . . . I keep my distance, *then* . . . I will be safe.

**Close Rangers**. If you are sensitive to rejection and fearful of bonds breaking, like to keep people nearby, are vigilant to changes in emotional temperature, and need a fair bit of reassurance that things are all okay, you may be a Close Ranger. It may be that Close Rangers' early caregiving was responsive, but it was not always predictably so: sometimes their needs were met, and sometimes they weren't. It was uncertain, so it was important for them to stay close and alert. And, unlike Lone Rangers, Close Rangers tend to centre the problem within, finding fault in and blaming themselves. They can be independent and fun loving, but when they sense conflict, separation or rejection, the strategies they use to cope with involve seeking greater proximity. They become focused on re-establishing emotional closeness and ruminating on worst-case scenarios.[41]

Imagine you meet up with your Close Ranger buddy just after they've had a first date.

'How did it go? Did you have fun?' you ask.

'I've texted her three times since I left the restaurant, but she hasn't written back, so obviously she isn't interested. Should I text again?' the Close Ranger might reply.

The Close Ranger needs contact to be reassured that all is well. Their blueprint mapping system looks a bit like this:

*If* . . . I stay close, *then* . . . I will feel safe.

**Roller Rangers**. If early caregiving was unpredictably responsive but with an added dimension of danger and punishment – when the 'safe' person could also be 'dangerous' – children grow up on uncertain footing. Part Lone Ranger, part Close Ranger, the Roller Rangers can experience relationships as tumultuous and, at times, bewildering. They find it hard to know where they stand, whether to trust or not, and how to read the safety signals, and so relationships can feel hard to navigate. If you find it tricky to make sense of what's what in relationships, not sure whether to stay close or run for the hills, you may be in this camp. Their blueprint mapping system looks a bit like this:

*If* . . . I stay vigilant, *then* . . . I will be safe.

It bears mentioning here that the experience of being betrayed can temporarily mimic the Roller Ranger experience – the safe person has, in a sudden turn, become dangerous, leaving you feeling bemused and disorientated.

\*\*\*

When Lone Rangers and Close Rangers get together, the push and pull of wanting and not wanting can create intense moments of connection but equally intense moments of pain. One wants more and the other wants less, closeness frightens one, distance frightens the other . . .

First date: the Lone Ranger is complimentary and self-assured, asking questions because this is comfortable territory in which they don't have to get too close. The Close Ranger finds this attractive as it indicates interest in them and a reassuring proximity – they want to be close, and so the dance begins. The Lone Ranger enjoys the excitement of the emerging relationship, because who doesn't? But once it looks as if it's heading towards commitment, echoes of their past templates are heard. They withdraw. But while the Lone Ranger is heading for the hills (often running), the Close Ranger becomes anxious, grabs the binoculars, gathers the hounds and calls in the SWAT team.

Roller Rangers too may take to the hills – also at quite a pace – but soon start to feel lost because they don't have any snacks and they left their compass behind. So back home they go. If their partner is *also* a Roller Ranger, they might return to find the fridge empty and the car gone. Neither knows what's going on, or where the other is. But if both parties just stay put and ride out their feelings of uncertainty, eventually they'll end up back at the ranch together and can settle down.

The key to success within all these pairings is solid communication. The Lone Rangers among you could always leave a note before running off, and the Close Rangers could read it and relax.

*I need some alone time.*

*I love you.*

*Back at 6p.m.*

While all this is going on, the Safe Harbours among you are looking on bemused at the comings and goings and wondering what all the fuss is about, but trusting it'll get resolved in time. The Safe Harbour knows that their Lone Ranger lover needs their alone time and will come back to them when they've had enough space, or that the Close Ranger needs a hug and reassurance. The Roller Ranger lover can circle round and round their Safe Harbour – who won't bat an eyelid.

So, if you're running for the hills, or waiting for the SWAT team to respond, or are tired and in need of a snack, try communicating your needs – with words. And if you find the Safe Harbours a little over-reliable in their ability to meet your needs, and somewhat lacking in the chemistry department (where's the dopamine hit?), don't dismiss them out of hand, because they might be just who you need – not only to feel safe, but to be safe.

At this point you may be trying to figure out which of these patterns fit you best. Humans don't naturally slot into neat categories – perhaps you have the capacity to feel more secure with certain people, or in certain communities, while in others, no matter how hard you try, you always feel on unsure footing. For the moment, focus on the relationship that has brought you here, and see if you can hear echoes of any of these patterns within it.

All of us develop early strategies to keep us feeling safe and confident within the dynamics of our relationships. They usually have a conditional ring to them – *if* ... *then* ... You may resonate with the strategies you've just heard from the Rangers, but yours may have a different flavour, emphasis, or an added specificity to them. See if you can identify what yours might be ... have a go. Here are some examples:

*If* ... I do what I'm told, *then* ... my parents won't be angry.

*If* ... I keep my feelings to myself, *then* ... I won't be teased.

*If* ... I stay in control, *then* ... there won't be any nasty surprises.

*If* ... I make people laugh, *then* ... they will be happy.

*If* ... I do what other people want, *then* ... I won't be rejected.

*If* ... I behave more like my sister, *then* ... I will be loved.

*If* ... I get angry, *then* ... I'll be punished.

Helpful as they were when you were young, these protective strategies can outlive their usefulness and, as we find ourselves in new situations, they can become restrictive, limiting our range of options to meet the needs of different social and emotional contexts.

# Chapter 9:
# The Dark Triad

There is one situation however where knowing your attachment pattern and protective strategies will provide you with no guidance . . . or protection. Because there are some people – charming, attractive and powerful – who are not playing by the usual rules. They are playing the game of the Dark Triad, the unholiest of unholy trinities – narcissism, psychopathology, Machiavellianism[42] – a major relationship red flag.[43]

NARCISSISM

PSYCHOPATHY                    MACHIAVELLIANISM

Very few people meet the clinical criteria for any one of these, let alone the full triumvirate, thank God. But the more of these traits that any individual possesses, the further away they are from the rule book. In fact, some of them have ripped it up completely and chucked it in the bin (or in your face).

Narcissists, with their inflated sense of their own importance and deep need for admiration and attention, hijack relationships with their high demands and impossible standards. Some narcissists present as very self-confident and demanding (grandiose narcissism), while others come across as self-conscious, withdrawn, and fragile-seeming (vulnerable or covert narcissism), but underneath is the same entitlement, superiority and antagonism.

Those on the psychopathic end are often highly intelligent, superficially charming, grandiose and manipulative. They tend to lack the capacity for remorse and shame, often ending relationships with little difficulty – what's not to love?

The Machiavels are a cunning and nasty bunch, duplicitous, scheming and unscrupulous. Indifferent to basic morality, they are often ruthlessly ambitious and will stop at nothing to get what they want.

No one sets out to fall for one of this lot . . .

But here's the thing. They are often extremely flattering, impressive, sexually confident, charming, well groomed and sometimes even rich and powerful. They make you believe it's you and them against the world, like Bonnie and Clyde (one hopes without the killings). They're the punchy types who think nothing of plugging their number into your phone, grabbing your coat and saying, 'Congratulations, you've pulled.'

People with this trinity of traits can often seem like 'The One' on account of the high chemistry they create, and when they turn their attention on you, it can be very difficult to resist. But it is a chemistry that rarely signifies love-ever-after despite the strong feelings to the contrary. Perhaps unsurprisingly they are more predisposed to infidelity[44] than others.

And they are exceptionally good at lying, something the rest of us are notoriously bad at detecting.

If you have been berating yourself for not spotting the signs sooner, for not reading clues, for not having suspicions that those late work drinks or trips abroad were anything other than innocent, and indeed for choosing the heartbreaker in the first place, you are not alone. These expert manipulators can go on weaving their intricate webs of deceit over months and years without detection. If they weren't able to charm and deceive, they might find themselves with few friends. They can more easily manage the physical symptoms that accompany their deceptions too – sweating, fidgeting, darting eyes. While most of us are more of the 'leaky liar' type[45], these experts can conceal their falsehood beneath a veneer of charm and seduction that would fool anyone.

So, if you fell in love with one of these charming love-bombers, don't judge yourself. And if you're not sure if you're with one, here are some key pointers:

You have stopped seeing your friends and family.
You feel insecure repeatedly.
Your needs are not being considered.
You're wondering if you've lost your mind.

Your version of events is constantly being undermined.

You want to end the relationship, but it feels impossible.

If you've identified with anything on this list (or everything on it), the first thing to know is that you are not alone and you are not losing your mind. But, you might be with someone who, no matter how hard you try – or wish it were otherwise – is never going to meet your needs. Bringing this into awareness for the very first time may be scary or even shocking. Or perhaps there is a sense of relief. Whatever comes up for you, don't judge it, let it be. We're here to help you navigate your way through this.

# Chapter 10:

# Identity

Before we continue, please make sure you have that photo of yourself from when you were a kid.

Now we're going to travel back in time for the next little while. Before we do, we would like you to create a safe place that will help you to feel grounded as we go on.

Find a comfortable position, either sitting or lying down, with your head, neck and spine aligned. Uncross your legs and let your hands rest in your lap or by your sides. We're going to ask you to use your imagination to create a place of deep relaxation and stillness.

Okay, let's begin by taking a few easy breaths, breathing in and breathing all the way out. Breathe in again, and this time see if you can send the warm energy of the breath to any part of your body that is tense, sore or tight and then release the tension with the exhale, breathing it all the way out. Do this a few times until you start to relax.

Any emotions and thoughts that are rocking around can be acknowledged and calmed with the breath, so that your emotional self is still and quiet, like a lake with no ripples.

Now imagine a place where you feel calm and peaceful and easy, a place from your past or somewhere you've always wanted to go. It doesn't matter where, just as long as it's a place that feels good, safe and peaceful. Allow the place to become real in your mind's eye. Look around and take it all in: the colours, the scenery, the smells and sounds. Feel the safety and peace of the place soaking into your skin, through the muscle and bone, all the way down to each and every cell, reaching the stillness at your very core.

Know that you can come back to this place of safety in your mind whenever you wish, to help your body and spirit relax simply by getting into a comfortable position and imagining yourself there.

***

So, with your journal in hand, find somewhere comfortable to sit. We want you to think back to a time before the age of ten when things felt difficult. And as you do, take a couple of long, deep breaths, in through your nose and out through your mouth, and allow all the tension to leave your body. Give yourself permission to relax. For a minute or two, just observe your breath, noticing how your belly rises on the inhale and falls back down as you breathe out. Allow your breath to flow freely, bringing you to a place of stillness. There is no rush; just be with your breath and observe the movements of your belly up and down. Allow any thoughts to come up and pass without judgement. All is well.

Think of the memory now and, as you do, we'd like you to see your younger self in this memory as if you were watching her on a television screen. Describe what you see in as much detail as you can. What is she doing? Who is she with? What is happening? What is she feeling? Give yourself time so the scene really comes alive.

Deep within you, the young girl you once were is waiting for you. She had needs that were not met and which you have long forgotten. She needed to feel safe and loved, to feel that she mattered, and that she could be herself.

Now I'd like you to imagine walking into the scene as the adult you are now: go and stand near her and introduce yourself. Tell her how pleased you are to see her, and gently ask her how she's feeling.

She's about to tell you something important. She's about to tell you how she feels about herself. Listen carefully, because she may find it difficult.

What is she telling you? (*I am . . .* ) Write the words down.

Bending down to her height now, and with all the warmth and compassion you can muster, tell her that you know she's been doing her best, that it's been really confusing for her, and that you have something to say about how you see her.

What do you tell her? (*You are . . .* ) Write the words down.

How does she respond? What is the expression on her face?
Does she say anything?

Take some time to enjoy this connection with her. You can let
her know that you will always be there for her.

When you're ready, gently bring your awareness back to your
breath and the sensations in your body. Take your time. You've
just done something important, generous and kind.

In that memory, the way you felt as a young girl represents the
fledgling belief you developed about yourself. What your adult
self told her is a new, flying belief infused with understanding
and empathy – altogether more represent-
ative of who you are. As an adult, you are
able to see what your younger self couldn't
see back then; that it wasn't her fault,
that she was doing her best, and that she
couldn't understand it all because she was
only a child.

ALICE

Take some time to write down your
memory and identify what your younger
self thought about herself (fledgling belief)
and what you as an adult told her about
herself (flying belief). Can you think what
you've done in your life to manage the
fledgling belief and keep yourself feeling

RUTH

safe? What kind of protective strategies did you develop? How might this have helped and hindered you in your life so far?

We're going to take a look now at your fellow guests' childhood memories and explore what was going on for them, how they navigated their close relationships and what strategies they developed to cope.

\*\*\*

READER: Before we go on, coming up next is one of those 'Dropping Anchor' moments we mentioned at the start of the book. If you're feeling upset by hearing the other women's stories as we go along, or in thinking about your own, remember that you can always 'Drop Anchor' to ground yourself.

\*\*\*

ESHE's memory:

> Eshe is eight or nine and dancing in the garden with her younger sister. Their parents are having a barbecue. There's music playing, people are smoking and drinking, and everyone is happy. She's holding hands with her sister, leaning back and spinning round and round, going faster and faster. All of a sudden, she's fallen over and there is a sharp pain to her head; she's on the ground and people are staring at her. Her dad rushes over and yanks her up, drags her inside by her hair, and everything goes deathly quiet. Eshe braces her-

self, covers her face. She knows what's coming, a hard thwack to her head, and he's shouting that she's ruined the party. She puts her hand up to her face and blood drips through her fingers – his ring must have caught her nose. She feels dizzy and faint and scared, and her dad is shouting at her to go to her room and stay there. Up in the bedroom, Eshe wants to lie down but is afraid she might stain the bedding, so she takes a tissue and presses it against her nose to stop the bleeding. She is shaking with pain and fear. She's angry too, with herself, with everyone, but most of all with her father. But as the bleeding subsides, and she begins to calm, she berates herself for being so clumsy, and blames herself. Why does she always ruin everything? She must try harder not to make her dad so angry. She vows never to let something like this happen again.

Eshe's early life was chaotic much of the time, and her father's drinking made him unpredictable and aggressive. She was never quite sure what his mood would be, but knew that more often than not his anger would escalate into violence. She was too young to understand then that he was an alcoholic, and she did her best to smooth things over and avoid punishment. She blamed herself, because at least this way she had some sense of control over the situation: if it was her fault then she could make it better by being and doing better. But the truth of it was that she was feeling alone, unloved and inadequate because she couldn't make it stop. Perhaps nobody noticed because on the outside she was good at appearing calm and cheerful, as though nothing could touch her, but inside she felt frightened and vulnerable, unsure if anyone was there for her at all.

Young Eshe told grown-up Eshe that she felt that she was 'no good. It's my fault that bad things happen.'

She developed a sensitive warning system to changes in atmosphere, and although she didn't always know what was needed, she tried not to make things worse, and to always appear cheerful so her dad wouldn't get angry.

*If* I'm careful . . . *then* things won't get worse.

*If* I'm cheerful . . . *then* people won't be angry.

Grown-up Eshe extended the strategy into her adult relationships and her intimate relationship with her betrayer, to gain a semblance of control.

And her strategies did keep her safe most of the time, but always trying to keep the peace meant her own needs disappeared from view and she became more and more lost, exhausted and disconnected from herself. And people didn't stop being angry. And when they did get angry at her, instead of calling time on the relationship, or leaving, she kept on trying to smooth things over, de-escalating the situation to make things feel safe.

When Eshe met her younger self, she told her that she was lovable, that she needed to be safe, and that it wasn't her fault. She told her little self that she was important and could ask for help.

*Eshe*

<u>Fledgling belief</u>: I'm no good. It's my fault that bad things happen.

<u>Protective strategy</u>: If I'm careful, then things won't get worse. If I'm cheerful, then people won't be angry.

<u>Unintended consequence</u>: I feel lost and disconnected and exhausted.

<u>Flying belief</u>: I'm lovable. It's not my fault. I'm important and can ask for help.

ROBYN's memory:

> Robyn is nine and her mother is holding up a large
> packet of sweets. Robyn's eyes are searching out the
> label, keen to identify which sweets they are, hoping
> they're her favourites – rhubarb and custard – but
> then she sees her mother's face looking like thunder
> and realises something is wrong because she only gets
> sweets on her birthday . . . and it's still May. And then
> it comes – her mother is accusing her of stealing them
> from the newsagents . . . but she's never seen the sweet
> packet before. Her stomach knots. She tells her mum
> she didn't steal the sweets, but her mother is convinced
> and claims she found the packet inside Robyn's school
> satchel and shows her where. Robyn knows she didn't
> put them in there and she knows she didn't steal them.
> Her mother is now ushering her out of the house, say-
> ing she has to take them back and apologise to the
> shopkeeper. As Robyn passes the stairs, she looks up
> to see her brother smirking. She starts to say some-
> thing, but her mother snaps at her to be quiet. Ben is
> two years older and has a temper to equal their moth-
> er's. She knows protest is hopeless, that he can do no
> wrong in their mother's eyes. She's been here many,
> many times before. Ten minutes later they are stand-
> ing in front of the shopkeeper, and her mother places
> the sweets on the counter and demands Robyn explain
> herself. Robyn knows it'll be over if she says sorry, but
> she's damned if she's going to apologise for something

she hasn't even done. She looks at the ceiling and then to the ground and imagines herself disappearing. Face and cheeks burning up, she turns on her heel and runs off, without looking back.

Robyn did what she needed to do to protect herself: she disconnected from those around her, and over time from herself. She grew up feeling helpless to advocate for herself and her truth, always batting it away, bullied by her brother and blamed by her mother. In her memory she told adult Robyn that she was feeling all alone and had no one on her side and that there was something bad about her, otherwise why would everyone be so unkind to her? As she grew up, she spent more and more time away from home or shutting herself off. She avoided other people to avoid getting hurt. As she entered adulthood, she discovered that alcohol made her feel better and helped her navigate the challenges of socialising, and particularly the emotional challenges of intimate relationships. But the unintended consequences of her withdrawal into alcohol was that she remained disconnected from those around her, a disconnect that ultimately hurt her more than it helped. She was always on the fringe of things, and was left by her unmentionable for the very strategy she'd employed to stay safe: for being distant.

When adult Robyn spoke to her younger self, she told her that she understood why she was scared and lonely.

She created a flying belief for her little self – that Robyn's feelings were important, and that she was brave and good.

## Robyn

*Fledgling belief:* I'm alone, no one's on my side, and I'm bad.

*Protective strategy:* If I disconnect and withdraw from others, then I won't be hurt.

*Unintended consequence:* But now I'm always on the outside feeling even more lonely and still being hurt.

*Flying belief:* My feelings matter, and I am brave and good.

NADIA's memory:

Nadia is six and her dad is taking her on an outing to his office in a huge building where he is a biology lecturer. It's the weekend and the building is empty. She is so happy to be there with him, just the two of them. There are two desks in his office, one for him and one for the other lecturer, whom Nadia hasn't met but has heard about. Nadia's dad has a chair that turns all the way around, and she's kicking off the ground and flying round on it. She is pretending to be a grown-up, answering the phone and pressing all the buttons so they light up.

A man comes in and Nadia feels something change. He is wearing a striped suit and thick glasses. Nadia thinks he must be very important and clever. Then she notices a boy that has come in with him. He's wearing a suit too, just like his dad's – 'How silly,' Nadia thinks. The important man is talking with her dad in low whispers. Nadia has no idea what they're talking about. The boy is now in the corner of the office examining a human skeleton and rattling off names of bones. Nadia hasn't heard of a lot of them, and he's oozing so much confidence over there in his suit, like a tiny teacher. The man is praising him, and her dad is now too: how clever he is to have remembered all those names. 'Maybe you'll be a professor one day,' his dad says to him. Nadia's dad turns to her, points to his head and says, 'You know this one . . .' Nadia knows because it's the head, of course, but then thinks maybe it has another name. Yes, it does, but she's forgotten it, so she says, 'It's your head.' The boy laughs. Her dad frowns but says encouragingly, 'Yes, but what's the bony structure called?' 'Face?' she offers tentatively, knowing already that she has got it wrong. The boy announces, 'Skull,' and Nadia wants to disappear. She pinches her hand hard under the desk to distract herself from the heat rising in her body. She wants to scream, and doesn't know what to do. She's feeling crushed and it's all the more acute because she had felt so confident and happy in the moments leading up to it.

On the way home, her dad doesn't say anything about the other man and the boy and the skeleton, and he doesn't mention it to her mum either when they get home. She's thinking he's pretending it didn't happen, and that he's embarrassed and disappointed with her. Nadia is unsure whether to mention it or not. She is feeling stupid for messing up, she's feeling terrible for letting her dad down in front of the clever man she felt it was important to impress.

To keep anything like this from happening again, she developed the protective strategy of asking lots of questions, knowing that her dad likes that, and in this way she won't disappoint him. And it works. Her parents tell her that curiosity is a wonderful quality, that it will serve her well in life, and she will go far, but inside she feels empty. Underneath all her questions, the experience at her dad's office settles into her. 'I'm stupid,' she tells herself.

Nadia knows she is lucky to have kind parents who are planning on sending her to a good school. They really love her. They are good, and she's done something shameful and maybe that means she doesn't deserve any of it. As she grows up, although people mostly seem pleased with her, underneath she is full of doubt and unsure of who she is or what she thinks – about anything.

Nadia was able to meet her younger self and tell her that she was capable, smart and has her own voice. She's trying on this new flying belief. It's difficult as she's so used to asking questions, but the group are helping her, gently teasing when she keeps asking them, and in this way challenging Nadia to stay with the uncertainty and trust that she may already have the answer.

# Nadia

<u>Fledgling belief</u>: I'm stupid and disappointing.

<u>Protective strategy</u>: If I ask lots of questions, no one will know I'm stupid and no one will be disappointed with me.

<u>Unintended consequence</u>: I'm always doubting myself and don't know who I am.

<u>Flying belief</u>: I am capable and smart, and I have a voice.

IRENE's memory:

Irene is seven years old and it's her mother's birthday. She's made a plan with her baby brother to make
their mum breakfast in bed as a birthday treat. They
have already been up to her bedroom with homemade
birthday cards, but she was fast asleep. It's now nearly
lunchtime and they are both in the kitchen. He's only a
babbling two-year-old, so isn't much help, but he loves
the sound the kettle makes when the water boils – hiss-
ing and whistling like a steam train. The kettle is blue
and shiny. Irene loves that it's shiny and keeps it pol-
ished so it stays that way. She's in charge, she's always
in charge these days. Her brother is crawling around
trying to mount the step stool Irene uses to reach for
everything, but he keeps falling down onto his bottom.
'He's such a baby,' Irene thinks. The toast pops and
Irene is buttering two slices when she hears a piercing
screech. For a split second she thinks it's the kettle . . .
She spins round and drops the plate. Her baby brother is thrashing around on the floor howling, his skin
turning redder by the second. Then she sees the empty
kettle beside him on the floor – and screams.

She can't move; it's as though her body is frozen in the
moment. Her mother comes hurtling down the stairs,
shouting at her to get to the neighbours' house for help.
Irene runs across the road, panicked and terrified,
and the next thing she remembers, the ambulance is

there, and her brother is being taken away along with her mum, still in her dressing gown. Irene thinks he's going to die, and when her mother doesn't come to pick her up from next door that night, she's sure he's dead, and she's sure it's her fault. When her mother returns to collect Irene the next day, she doesn't say anything about her brother, and goes straight up to her bedroom. It's a day later that Irene finds out from the neighbour that her brother is still in hospital but he's alive. Her mother isn't talking to her, and it remains that way for some time.

Irene was too young to understand then that her mother was depressed, not just because her father was so often away with the army – which is what she'd always say when Irene asked her what was wrong – but because he was having an affair and threatening her with divorce. Instead, Irene thought it must be her fault that her mother was so quiet and down, and it was certainly her fault that her brother got hurt. 'I'm incompetent and can't be trusted,' she thought to herself, not able to understand that she should never have been put in that position of responsibility in the first place. She decided that she must be more careful, plan everything really well and defer to others who knew better than her.

And this felt safer. But this strategy had unintended consequences in her life and in her relationships. There was a kind of innocence to her. She never took any risks. And she undermined her own achievements, always claiming to be lucky rather than competent, and so never really *felt* capable – even though she clearly was. She rarely trusted her own feelings and in her long marriage deferred to Stan, and in doing so kept things stable, but often at the expense of her own needs and desires. She kept saying what a good life she'd had, and the group gently reminded Irene that she can have had a good life, *and* there could have been difficulties. The two statements can co-exist – they'd say – reminding Irene of the dialectic.

What her older self saw and knew when she went back into the memory was that Irene was capable, and full of fun and passion. Her brother's burns were not her fault, but nobody had told her that. She can trust herself . . . it was an accident.

## Irene

<u>Fledgling belief</u>: I can't trust myself.

<u>Protective strategy</u>: If I'm careful and plan well, and if I defer to others, then everyone will be safe.

<u>Unintended consequence</u>: I don't feel capable or know what I want.

<u>Flying belief</u>: I am capable and full of fun and passion. I can trust myself.

LIN's memory:

> Lin found the exercise too challenging, and she felt unable to go into any memory before the age of ten years. She couldn't connect with who she was as a child and had no sense of what she might have been like. The group tried to help her create a picture of the little girl she once was, given the incredible woman she is now, but Lin just wept, unable to take in anything they said. None of it felt real or solid to her.

> Lin approached Alice during the break and told her how wretched she was feeling, that she can't do it properly, and that she's now worried she won't get to where the other women have got to and won't feel any better when she leaves.

# Chapter 11:
# The Rabbit

**Scene III**

**COSY DEN. LATE NEXT MORNING.**

The women are ALL gathered and ALICE *turns to* LIN.

ALICE:    How about we start from a different place? How about you tell me what you liked doing as a kid?

LIN:    Okay, I do remember that I loved being in the garden and watching the butterflies.

ALICE:    Do you remember what your garden was like?

LIN:    It was a small garden with a banyan tree that I climbed, and we had a rabbit hutch at the back. I was always busy with the rabbit, and making sure the hutch was clean and cosy.

ALICE: You had a rabbit?

LIN: Yes.

ALICE: What kind of rabbit was it?

LIN: She was brown and fluffy. She was really small. A dwarf rabbit, tiny.

ALICE: Did she have a name?

LIN: Cookie.

ALICE: Good name. Tell me about Cookie . . .

LIN: She was so soft, like velvet. I loved stroking her and feeding her. I'm sure I wasn't supposed to give her so much food, but she didn't mind and I loved giving her treats. And she was always trying to escape.

ALICE: She sounds adorable. Were you the one who looked after her?

LIN: Yes, it was mostly me, sometimes it was my sister, but she was more into petting her than looking after her. I cleaned out the hutch, fed her, filled the water bottle and brushed her fur, although thinking back now I'm not sure she liked it much, but I loved brushing her. Sometimes I put her in my school bag and pretended to take her on little trips . . . actually she was probably my best friend.

ALICE:   It sounds as though you really loved her, Lin, and looked after her so well. Can I just check in with how you're feeling as you're telling me about little Cookie?

LIN:   Happy and sad at the same time . . . I guess thinking about her as my best friend makes me feel sad; it makes me remember how lonely I was.

ALICE:   I get that, you felt really lonely, and you had a lot of love to give, which you gave to Cookie. And you did a great job looking after her. It was good that you had her. And I'm sorry you felt so alone. As you think about that memory now, petting and looking after Cookie, can you tell me a bit more about you, the little girl in the memory with her rabbit? What's she like?

LIN:   She's really cute. I can see that she has her hair in bunches. She's actually really good at looking after Cookie, and has fun with her. She's resourceful, playful . . . and kind . . . [crying but smiling through the tears]. She's happy playing with Cookie.

ALICE:   I agree, she sounds really cute, and resourceful and kind and fun. Cookie was lucky to have her.

# Lin

Fledgling belief: I'm alone, and no one will protect me.

Protective strategy: If I hide myself, don't let anyone else in, do well and focus on others, then I'll be safe.

Unintended consequence: I'm cut off from myself, my needs and my desires.

Flying belief: I'm cute, resourceful, playful and kind.

POSTSCRIPT: Thinking about a happy memory was what Lin needed to do to be able to see her younger self. It was only later that day that Lin told us that she had been sexually abused by her uncle when she was five years old and that she thinks her mother knew about it. She had kept this memory hidden for so long, and it was so frightening to think about, that most of her memories from that time had also gone – blanked out to keep herself safe. That is how she survived the abuse growing up, but it was also why as an adult she felt lost. She hid who she was, scared of letting anyone get too close. She kept her focus on others, and did her very best in both her working life (as a radiologist) and in her relationship with her partner. But in the process, she lost herself. The route back for Lin was through connecting to a good memory, which enabled her to connect with herself as a kid. She knew who she was, even if it was hard for her to get there.

How about you? Were you able to get to your fledgling belief and strategies? How did you find going into a childhood memory? We invite you to make notes along the lines of your fellow guests to help you identify what sense you made of your early nest and how you've navigated your subsequent relationships. Have there been unintended consequences in adulthood resulting from your childhood strategies?

# Chapter 12:
# You're Precious

**Scene IV**

**COSY DEN. EARLY AFTERNOON**

> *After lunch, ROBYN had felt so overwhelmed that she had got into her car to leave, but at the driveway changed her mind and came back. She went to find RUTH and told her why she had wanted to leave. The group are now all gathered and ready to begin.*

RUTH: Robyn has been feeling really overwhelmed, so much so that she almost left after lunch, but even though she's scared, she's here now and ready to share something with you all.

*[ROBYN stares at the ceiling, as if in another world, or trying to escape this one, her leg jiggling, she's clearly in distress. RUTH gently asks if she's okay and if she needs*

*anything. RUTH goes to ROBYN, wraps a blanket round her shoulders and gives her a hug.]*

ROBYN:   It was in my last year of primary school. I was ten. My class got free swimming lessons for a term, and I was so excited because I'd never been to the local pool and always envied our neighbours who went every Saturday. Mum somehow managed to scrape together the money for my costume and I loved it – shiny red with criss-cross straps at the back. It felt so grown up. I wore that swimsuit underneath my school uniform every day before our first lesson. The swimming coach told me I was a natural but said that I needed goggles if I was going to keep coming. I didn't want to tell him the truth – that we couldn't afford them – so I said I'd lost them. He told me not to worry and that he'd bring a pair along next time. He gave me a pair of brand new goggles at the start of our second lesson and molested me in the changing rooms afterwards ... I've never told anyone ... [*looks down and covers her face in her hands*].

ALICE:   Robyn, I'm so sorry to hear this happened to you, and you must have been really scared. It's not at all uncommon for children not to tell anyone, because they are frightened. I know this is not a place where you want to stay, and we won't stay any longer than we have to. You are an adult now, and it's not happening now, but let's slow it down a little. See it as if it was happening on a TV screen, can you see the little you? Do you remember how she felt?

ROBYN: I can.

ALICE:   What is she feeling?

ROBYN: Scared.

ALICE:   I'm sure she is, it was really scary. How did she cope with feeling that scared?

ROBYN: She just kept it all to herself and tried to forget.

ALICE:   She was very resilient, and I'm thinking that must have felt really lonely for her . . .

ROBYN: She was so lonely, she just went into her own little bubble and shut everyone out.

ALICE:   Because there was no one there she could trust.

ROBYN: No one [*face in hands as the tears finally come*].

ALICE:   Stay with it for a little longer . . . with all this going on, what was little Robyn feeling about herself?

ROBYN: That she was all alone and no one cared. That she was nothing.

ALICE:   That must have been so hard . . . If you keep her in mind for a moment longer, see if you can step into the scene as the wise adult you are now, reach out to her, and take her by the hand. And now as you feel that strength you have as an adult, take her with you, out of the scene and somewhere safe.

[*Pause*]

Where do you take her?

ROBYN: To the small park near my house.

ALICE:  And still holding her hand now, how is she feeling there with you in the park?

ROBYN: Better . . . She's relieved [*sobbing*].

ALICE:  Good, she's got you now, she'll never be alone again.

[*Pause*]

Can you look at me for a moment? You've just done a brave and kind thing, and whenever your little self feels alone and scared, you can look after her anytime. You can take her hand and bring her to the park where she can be with you while she's upset, where she can feel safe.

ROBYN: That feels good actually, I can imagine that.

ALICE:  And while you're imagining that, speaking to the part of her that feels as though she's nothing, what would you say?

ROBYN: I'm here. You're safe, you're precious [*smiling through her tears*].

# Chapter 13:

# Power and Shame

It is, and always has been, that those with power influence the identity of those without it and assign the rules of engagement to which the less powerful must adhere. This power dynamic is woven into the fabric of every family, institution, organisation, culture, religion and social environment – and it is the over-arching framework within which we learn who we are. This hierarchy of power is the backdrop to your heartbreak.

Fitting on that tiny glass slipper was the only thing standing between Cinderella and her happily-ever-after. The 'ugly' sisters' feet were on the larger side and the slipper didn't fit. Only Cindy with those tiny, tiny toes could get the slipper on and marry her prince. Throughout history, women have been rejected and shamed for having bodies – or feet – that don't fit the cultural prescription of beauty. As Cinderella discovered, having small feet was her route out of servitude and into freedom, power and status. The idea of the diminutive equating to feminine attractiveness is as pervasive as it is shaming.

Your feet are just your feet. The value system telling you how your feet are supposed to look is what creates the shame.

The stories about who women are and where they rank go back a long, long way. The story of Adam and Eve is often called the story of original sin, and, surprise, surprise, it was Eve's fault. Weak Eve (for being tempted by the serpent). Wicked Eve (for being hungry). Fast forward a few thousand years and we're being burnt as witches (a wart on the face was enough to qualify), discarded at birth for not being male (no vaginas here, thanks), and shamed for menstruating (standard). This global historical and cultural context situates and infuses the experience of women – before we're even born.

The psychological fallout from all of this is pervasive and painful and attacks the very core of your self-worth with a narrative that whispers, 'You are worth less,' and 'Shame be upon you'. With disempowerment comes invalidation, and sadly this is the plight of women all over the world.

Controlling the conversation, trivialising, dismissing, punishing, ignoring, humiliating, shaming, denying, manipulating – these are the mechanisms through which power *can* be exercised. It sounds a bit like this . . .

*You're not thinking clearly . . .*

*You know you sound insane right now . . .*

*You're making a big deal out of nothing as always . . .*

*You can't take a joke . . .*

*You take everything so personally . . .*

*You're being oversensitive . . .*

*You're overthinking this . . .*

*It's your fault, not mine . . .*

*I never said that . . .*

*You're the problem here, not me . . .*

*I haven't got time for this . . .*

*I'm doing this because I love you . . .*

*Why would you think that?*

*This says more about you than me . . .*

*It's your fault I cheated; you're not hot enough . . .*

*It didn't happen like that . . .*

*You're making it up . . .*

*You're irrational . . .*

*You're wrong . . .*

*You're always getting it muddled . . .*

*What's the matter with you?*

*You need therapy . . .*

*Are you really going to wear that?*

*You used to be fun . . .*

*It's not important . . .*

*It doesn't matter . . .*

*It didn't happen . . .*

And to minimise the threat posed by such gaslighting, the following strategies are often employed to manage it: self-surveillance, self-blame, deference, self-silencing, tolerance of 'misbehaviour', appeasement, compliance, withdrawal, body hating, overeating, undereating, ruminating, self-harm, self-criticism and self-punishment. It looks like this . . .

*If you lost weight they might give you the time of day, and be sure to think twice before you speak up in case it provokes them . . .*

*Be totally cool with the odd affair . . .*

*Don't complain if they don't empty the dishwasher, they've had a hard day, after all, and tell them they look wonderful so they don't hit you . . .*

*Ruminate on how to do better and be sure to buy the latest self-help book and brutalise your body at the gym . . .*

*Look over your shoulder, stay safe . . .*

*Cry if you must (but only into your pillow, lest you disturb their sleep) . . .*

*Drink gallons of wine and, with any luck, you'll forget . . .*

*Don't tell anyone they're treating you badly . . . because it's all your fault . . .*

*Back down or go down . . .*

*Put out or shut up . . .*

*Sympathise and empathise with all their problems and make excuses for them . . . because it's not easy being them.*

None of us would really give this advice, nor do we set out to be in relationships where we operate like this, yet we can all see ourselves reflected somewhere here. This is what happens when you're on the losing side of the power dynamic. And it is these everyday micro-betrayals that magnify your heartbreak, the ongoing accumulation of which adds up to extreme frustration, diminished agency, shame and negative self-worth (Hwa-Byung, even).

This toxic mix is felt in the body – heat in the cheeks, stirring in the stomach, dry mouth, downcast eyes, sinking posture, nausea. Your body is always the first responder, tightening around shame and invalidation, colluding to keep it secret. You retreat inside yourself and time slows down as you try to disconnect and hide from what's happening, willing it all to go away. And in this hidden place, the shame can attach to your early fledgling beliefs like a limpet.

But the truth is, none of this has got anything to do with who you are and has everything to do with the definitions that those in power give you in order to maintain the status quo. They were never your definitions in the first place. Not when you were a child and not now as an adult. They belong to those who have sought to control you.

When you are rejected or replaced or cheated on, when the person you love and trust chooses someone else over you, the shame is on them. And if your heartbreaker tries to manipulate you into believing it's the other way around (*You're not seeing it from my perspective; you never stick up for me; you're always making me feel small; you never cared about what I needed; you don't value my opinion; you love the kids more than me and always put them first*), don't take it on. Their shame is not yours to feel – it belongs to them.

Shame will tell you to bury all the evidence lest you expose the faults that lie deep within you (or your feet). And this creates problems. It's lonely keeping secrets, it disconnects you from others, and it takes energy to keep them suppressed. So, let's turn it around, connect with others and start sharing our 'shameful' secrets. Ruth and I find it very bonding to share the fact we both have large feet, and laugh about the ways they have defined us. How has the shape and size of your feet (or any other body part) shaped how you think about yourself as a woman? #bigfeetarebeautifultoo

Social and physical shaming is a mechanism used by those in power to discredit entire groups of people on account of their gender, race, sexual orientation, education, religion, language, income, immigration status, ability. *Shame be upon you* for your being different to those in power.

Women can be diminished in many underhand and subtle ways that gradually become internalised – *drip drip drip* – until what you have been told about yourself becomes indistinguishable from who you think you are.

*You're a bit of a show off.*
    #justexpressingmyself
*Are you on your period?*
    #beingawoman
*You asked for it.*
    #metoo
*You're boring.*
    #imtired
*You're always tired.*
    #fightingthepatriarchyisexhausting

One of the hardest kinds of subordination to spot is the backhanded compliment – flattering yet simultaneously invalidating.

It's subordination disguised as sweet talk, delivering an unpleasant sting that can be tricky to pin down.[46]

*You look so great in that photo; I didn't recognise you at first.*
(Inference: You usually look rough.)
*I wish I could be so relaxed about all this clutter.*
(Inference: You're a slob.)
*You scrub up well.*
(Inference: You look like shit most of the time.)
*Ooh, you look so comfy in that outfit.*
(Inference: I wouldn't be seen dead in it.)
*I wish I had as much time on my hands as you do.*
(Inference: You're lazy.)
*Your house is so cosy.*
(Inference: You're poor with no style.)
*You're coping so much better than I thought you would.*
(Inference: You're usually on the verge of a nervous breakdown.)
*Your hair looks good today.*
(Inference: It's a bird's nest most of the time.)

When we adopt the lens of those who seek to disempower and weaken us, it not only brings *us* down, it brings *all women* down. Recognising these messages for what they are – instruments of invalidation – is the first step towards breaking free of them. These barbed insults in disguise are designed to keep you in your place. They are not the truth.

We know that shame can be hard to spot; it's often present just outside of view when you're feeling terrible about yourself, when you want to avoid or withdraw from others, when you are ruminating on your mistakes, when you're feeling fearful of rejection or being found out, when you are feeling exhausted, defeated and reaching for the wine. Bring your shameful secrets out into the light by telling someone you trust. Write them down and burn the paper, take whatever steps you need to rid yourself of them. Let your feet be your feet . . . and be proud.

Have a think back to the work you did on your childhood self. Is the shame you feel now connected to your early nest experience and your fledgling beliefs? Chances are, the shame you are feeling may be linked to early life experiences; perhaps it was a parent, teacher, school bully, sibling, first love or religious leader who invalidated you, and if so, it's important you leave it with them.

# PART III:

# The Future

# Chapter 14:
# Handing it Back

We are going to take you through an exercise now that will set the intention and context in which you will start to rethink who you are. We've been into the past and dismantled some of the scaffolding of your early thoughts and behaviours and now we need to clear some space for something new and purposeful to emerge.

Okay. Find a comfortable position, sit back and relax. The first part is a meditation; we invite you to read it through a few times before closing your eyes and faithfully taking yourself through the steps and imagining it.

Take a deep breath and feel the tension leave your body as you settle into a place of self-reflection and healing.

Take another deep breath and another, and be aware that with each breath you take, you become more deeply relaxed and at ease.

Feel yourself drifting, peaceful and relaxed, deeper and deeper into a comfortable place within yourself.

You can feel yourself becoming more relaxed now with each new breath.

Your body is breathing a sigh of relief as you just let go and settle into a deeper sense of ease and comfort.

Your mind and heart are becoming free from worry, and a warm, peaceful sensation is spreading within your chest.

You can feel your entire body breathing a sigh of comfort and relief, as you drift further and further into a deep, soothing peace. Just allow any tension you find to be there, and feel it slowly drifting away.

Now imagine a circle of warm, soft light at the top of your head.

Slowly feel that circle expand to spread across your head and face, soothing and caressing your skin as it gently relaxes all of the muscles in your face and forehead.

Feel the warm waves of relaxation continuing to drift easily and naturally down into your neck, then quietly spreading across your shoulders.

Notice the tension leaving your body as you take another deep, cleansing breath.

The mild, comforting waves of relaxation are spreading down your arms and across your chest now, washing away any distress, tension or discomfort that was there.

Your entire torso is feeling more comfortable and relaxed now, as the waves of comfort and ease spread further down your body.

Your hips and stomach are feeling the relaxation spread and

wash through them, bringing soothing comfort naturally and easily into your upper legs and thighs.

As this feeling of letting go continues, notice how it slowly spreads across and around your knees, your lower legs and calves.

Now the warm waves of relaxation are reaching your feet, and you notice how all of the tension that was in your upper body is leaving through your toes, giving you a general sense of quiet, calm and ease.

Now imagine that you are seeing yourself at a much, much younger age, somewhere before the age of ten years old.

You are totally safe and in charge as you travel back to see your younger self again.

We'd like you to imagine her outside, somewhere by the sea perhaps, or on a mountain or in a park or woodland, and picture the scene around you. What can you see? What can you smell? What can you hear? In your mind's eye you see that the little girl that is you is wearing a jumper over her clothes. And on that jumper, you can see that something has been written. And when you look closely, you see that it is the fledgling belief you were given about yourself.

Now, gently and lovingly, we want you to ask your younger self to remove the jumper and hand it over to you.

You and your younger self both turn and in the distance you can see the person who gave you that fledgling belief. On behalf of your younger self, you approach this person and give them the jumper; you hand back the fledgling belief that was never yours.

As you do, you gently say to this person, 'I forgive you. I'm sorry for your pain.' And invite them to hand the jumper back to whoever it was that gave it to them.

In this way, the belief gets handed back across the generations.

Now turn back to your younger self. She's been waiting and watching patiently.

As you lovingly approach her, you hand her a new jumper and ask her to put it on. You can help her if you like.

Once she has it on, you both see that it has something written on it – the new, updated, flying belief that you created for your little self.

Read it, savour the way it sounds, the way it makes you feel to give her this flying, flourishing belief, and notice the expression on her face as she takes it in.

Give her a big hug now and tell her, 'You are loved. You are seen. You are understood.'

Spend as much time as you like in this hug. Feel how good it is to be in contact with her. Tell her that you will always protect her, always care for her, and always give her what she needs. She doesn't even have to ask.

We'd like you to focus on your breath again now and become gently aware of the sounds around you and the present moment. And, when you are ready, give yourself a nod of acknowledgement that you have had this experience and taken part in something deeply compassionate that is larger than yourself, and in so doing contributed to healing the heartbreaking ancestral echoes that extend far beyond your own heartbreak.

# Chapter 15:

# Emotional Regulation

Whatever you are feeling right now is okay: let it be. You will come to see that you need all of your feelings, that they are signals from your body that help you orientate and understand what's needed.

Feelings have a shared trajectory. They peak and trough, ebb and flow, come and go. Some stay around for longer, others are brief, but like the tides they have a natural pulsation, in and out. What they don't do is intensify forever. Still, when those difficult feelings do intensify, you might find yourself wanting to short-circuit them. A glass of wine (or a bottle), the Instagram-a-thon, a sugar-induced sofa coma, we've all been there. And getting away from feelings does create short-term relief, but in the long term, burying, avoiding or cutting yourself off from them will lead you to believe that they're unmanageable, frightening and leave you bereft of the vital information they contain. So have them and let them do their job – which is to guide you.

You need all your feelings, even the ones you don't like. They are important and necessary and serve a purpose. If you feel angry, there has been an injustice. If you feel afraid, that signals danger. And if you feel calm, there is safety and connection.

Your feelings are your internal barometer telling you when you need to act and when you don't. We have three emotional systems that work together to guide us: Defend, Drive and Recover.[47] Each is important and necessary, and it is through the three working together in a balanced way that emotional equilibrium is reached and maintained.

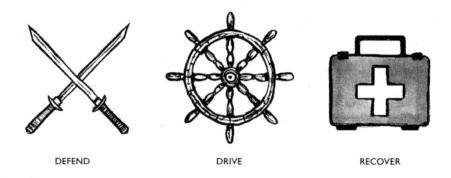

DEFEND                    DRIVE                    RECOVER

Our **Defence** system is our red zone, flashing to alert us to danger. To keep ourselves safe, this system uses powerful feelings such as anger, fear and disgust to charge our bodies with cortisol and adrenaline hormones so that we can protect ourselves from danger. But there are many other things we can feel that also make us believe we are under threat. Here are some of them.

**DEFEND**

RED ZONE

Programmed over millennia, **Defence** is the most dominant of our three emotional systems, and is extremely sensitive to threat from both the external landscape (lions, heartbreakers, muggers), and internal (images, thoughts, memories). It's like having your own sentry guard on permanent watch alerting you whenever something seems wrong – physically, morally or emotionally – and triggering your survival responses: fight, flight, freeze or fawn.

Think of a cat-and-mouse chase. The tiny mouse first tries to outrun the quick-witted cat, scampering about at breakneck speed, its **Defence** system in overdrive – this *flight* response is the mouse's super-skill. After all, it's not going to come out well in a *fight* against its feline enemy, so on it runs, under, over, this way and that. But the cat just keeps on coming at it, paw after paw, pounce after pounce, and before long the mouse is going to be completely exhausted. But the little mouse has one final option, a last resort, and it's a very clever one. It goes completely limp. It mentally checks out and feigns death – if it's going to be eaten it may as well be unconscious when it happens. The mouse *freezes*. Confused by this sudden turn of events, the cat paws at the mouse's immobile body, willing it to move so the chase can start up again – it's the chase the cat loves (mean, isn't it?) – but to no avail. Kitty eventually gets bored and wanders off in search of a livelier victim to taunt, at which point the mouse 'comes to' and makes good its escape.

Like the mouse, you too have all these responses. But, unlike the mouse, you have an extra superpower – the ability to *fawn*, to make friends with the enemy. You can read the social and emotional cues in a dangerous situation and use your relational knowledge to talk your way out. You can cast your eyes to the ground, flatter, apologise, agree, and in any number of ways make yourself unobjectionable and non-threatening to mitigate danger and enact a *fawn* response. If only the mouse knew a joke or two.

Our **Drive** system, the blue zone, propels us towards achieving what we want and need. Associated with feelings of excitement, purpose and agency, it's our pleasure and prosper mechanism, alerting us to what's possible and giving us the energy to achieve it. This is where our energy and hope lie, where we feel most alive. **Drive** is fulfilled when what you're doing is aligned with what you want, knowing all the while that **Defend** is available when you need it. When this system is guiding us, our body is flooded with dopamine, and we feel happy, motivated, alert and focused.

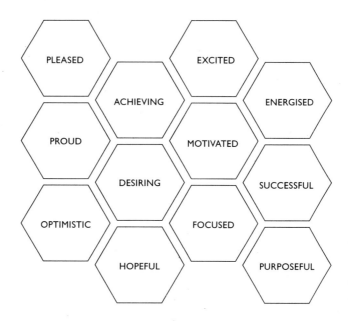

**DRIVE**
BLUE ZONE

PLEASED

EXCITED

ACHIEVING

ENERGISED

PROUD

MOTIVATED

DESIRING

SUCCESSFUL

OPTIMISTIC

FOCUSED

HOPEFUL

PURPOSEFUL

Our **Recovery** system, the green zone, is all about feeling warm, peaceful and contented. It has a safe and unworried vibe – a cocoon of connection. Oxytocin and endorphins flood our bodies as we rest and recharge our batteries, leaving us feeling soothed and ready for anything. When **Defend** and **Drive** are guiding us, our bodies are charged and active, but when we are in **Recovery** mode, our bodies are able to digest all those active hormones and return to a more peaceful, calm and settled state of being.

We need to feel safe in order to sink into the green zone. No one can set about resting and recovering while there is danger. For all animals, humans included, physical and emotional safety is a prerequisite for us to let down our guard, discharge all those high-energy hormones, and replenish our emotional and physical tanks. The fullest expression of the green zone is when we are in connection with others, feeling accepted, supported and loved. Self-help is good, but together-help is even better.

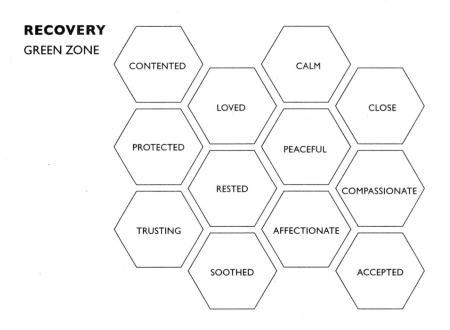

**RECOVERY**
GREEN ZONE

CONTENTED    CALM    LOVED    CLOSE    PROTECTED    PEACEFUL    RESTED    COMPASSIONATE    TRUSTING    AFFECTIONATE    SOOTHED    ACCEPTED

If The Heartbreak Hotel was a colour, it would be green.

It is our green system that we often give the least attention to. In our high-pressured, fast-paced, striving culture, we rarely give ourselves permission to be in green. So let's help each other get there. We'll put money on your being better at *greening* for others than you are for yourself, so you definitely know how. And if someone wants to help you, keep in mind the pleasure you feel when someone asks *you* for help and offer them that same experience in return. Because when someone offers to be there for you, they are *greening* for you – it is a communication of care and kindness, an act of love. If you're someone who worries about being a burden on others, think of it like this – by not asking for help you are robbing someone of the pleasure they would have experienced from being needed and valued by you.

Heartbreak is an emotionally dysregulating experience of great magnitude, your red system is flashing neon with fear and anger, green is nowhere to be seen, and blue has been thrown overboard by your heartbreaker. You're struggling to find *any* green, unable to sleep, let alone rest – and we understand this. But no amount of trying to motivate yourself out of your feelings, or propelling yourself onwards before you are ready, is going to get you to where you want to go. Take a rest instead . . . a short rest will leave you much stronger physically and emotionally than any amount of screen time . . . or wine.

Most people still find this difficult despite feeling completely exhausted. While relaxation can take many forms – running, meditation, yoga or hanging out with friends, for example – green is best when it's a low-stimulation activity, something peaceful and quiet. The brain and body need downtime, so avoid anything that will put you back into a **Drive** mode. Screens may be relaxing, but they do not qualify as rest. And rest is never lazy, rather it is a necessary prerequisite for you to gather your strength. Think of it as an investment in your future. And if the idea of silence makes you nervous, try gentle music in its place, or if you are struggling to sleep, know that the simple act of being quiet and keeping still in a dark room is restorative.

If you're currently feeling masses of red, if you're worrying about your feelings overwhelming you, or feeling completely overwrought by the whole business of your heartbreak, here are a few more techniques you can use to help bring the temperature down and enable you to think more clearly.

**Balloon Breathing**

Place your hand on your belly.

Imagine that your belly is a balloon.

Take a deep breath and fill that balloon with air.

Then, exhaling slowly, deflate the balloon.

Now close your eyes and really feel that balloon inflating and deflating as you continue to breathe.

As you feel more and more relaxed – and when you're ready – breathe out and let the balloon slowly drift away into the sky.

## The Butterfly Hug

Cross your hands over your chest, palms facing inwards, and link your thumbs.[48]

Make sure your middle fingers are resting lightly on your collarbone.

Raise your elbows to create your butterfly wings.

Slowly tap your hands on your chest, alternating left and right.

While tapping, breathe in through your nose and out through your mouth until you feel calm.

What sits behind the butterfly hug, and the reason it's so effective, is the principle of bilateral stimulation. It turns out there is a kind of magic to be found in the simple rhythmic movements of our bodies. And it's not limited to the butterfly hug. Jogging, walking, banging on drums, anything that involves alternating movements can qualify.

This was discovered by chance by psychologist Francine Shapiro, during a walk in a park. She noticed that some distressing feelings she was having suddenly stopped. She realised that walking while she was thinking about them helped her to feel better, beyond the expected benefits of the fresh air and aerobic exercise. Bilateral stimulation activates both sides of the brain, allowing it to better process information, something your brain does naturally during REM sleep, which can help distressing memories settle down.

You may have built bilateral stimulation into your daily life in ways you're unaware of. When you alternate taps on the steering wheel or tap your arms or legs to music and find yourself somehow soothed; when you decide to go for a walk to 'clear your head', it's the bilateral stimulation that does it. Utilise the restorative power of bilateral stimulation, and let your body do the processing for you in any way you like. Practise getting into green through your body – and your mind will follow.

# Chapter 16:

# The Compass

The wider world around you will always have a view about what you should be doing, and what or who you should want, what success looks like, and what you *really* need. Some of it may be worth listening to, but a lot of it isn't. The clamour of competing voices directs our wants and desires every time we switch on our phones. The algorithms in the ether push and pull us this way and that, promising us happiness and fulfilment if only we buy their latest gadget, drink their Kool-Aid, pop their pill, join their club, and follow them because, well ... everyone else is.

***

Heartbreak changes futures, often obliterating them. Your plans, dreams, certainties and hopes may have altered radically and left you with a sense of swirling uncertainty and groundlessness. We get that. But we are now moving into a different space in which you will reimagine your future, returning once more to what you really love and want. We're not going to approach this by looking at things in a linear fashion. There's nothing more daunting than seeing a vast expanse of time stretching before you and thinking you have to make a plan for it right away. Instead, we're going to focus only on now – the present. Each decision you make in the present moment creates your future.

Futures unfold – they don't already exist.

What matters to you? What do you want and need? It may have been a very long time since you last asked yourself this, especially if you have spent many years in service to others.

Let's take that time now.

Values are not concrete; they are more like important principles through which you can articulate your next steps. They are not the same as goals, which usually have an end point, rather they are your direction of travel. Values endure – they cannot be completed or achieved. They are ways of living, ideals if you like, characterised by fullness, purpose and vital engagement. Think of them as foundations shoring up a home: it'll always be steady if it's built on solid ground. Any goals you create for yourself in the future will be infused by your values – like a drop of lemon in a glass of water.

Let's first deal with the imperatives of 'should', 'must' and 'ought'. They are commanding and authoritative, ordering you around in an aggressive and often tyrannical way. We use them to get ourselves or others to do things we don't want to do. We'd like you to consider these imperatives very lightly as we go on, preferably bracketing them off completely. Imperatives are usually coming from other people's expectations of you, and they may not be in your best interests.

In their place, we want your own needs and desires to come into play. Less of the imperative and more of the inquisitive.

Remember we said we'd never ask you to do something we hadn't done ourselves? Well, it was identifying our own values that led us here, to you . . .

**ALICE.** After my mother died, I was thrown into a disoriented, lost state of feeling, like being a child again. I'd spent almost a decade looking after my mum, alongside bringing up young children, teaching and running a private practice. It occurred to me in the first few weeks of grief that over the previous decade I had gone from being someone who felt I knew who I was and what made me tick, to being completely at a loss. It was all a big mess in my head, with no clear way through. I was on compassionate leave from my various professional roles but couldn't find any energy or forward motion.

So I did what I had asked many, many of my clients to do in their times of disorientation. I did a values clarification exercise. And in doing it I realised this: I needed to laugh more and have more joy in my life, I wanted to honour the introvert that I am with more solitude and quietness, I needed to reconsider the relationships in my life and nurture the connections that were nourishing for me. And I wanted more abundance and fullness in my life and to keep learning.

Nearly three years on, I am happier, more fulfilled. Not because I set out to be, but because the grief showed me that I needed to get back to myself, and because, through making decisions aligned with my values, I now have a more joyful, meaningful and connected life. The consequence of ignoring what mattered to me had pretty much led me to burnout and exhaustion. Looking back at that period now, the period before my mum died, I had come very far from myself, and was suffering as a result. Grief and the disorientation it brought was the catalyst to get back together with myself.

**RUTH.** Alice was convinced of the transformative value of this exercise, something she had recently done herself. She was passionate about it and I was intrigued because she seemed different – more energised and purposeful – and I wanted a piece of the action! It wasn't easy, but I did it.

What came up for me was how much I wanted to help others. I had been writing a novel, but the prospect of finding an audience for it was getting slimmer. I enjoyed writing very much, but I wasn't sure I was being driven by what was really important to me. I wrote down my values in the front of my journal to help keep me focused and oriented towards what I decided then mattered to me most: compassion, connection, commitment, grace.

Having them close always keeps me moving in the right direction, and, as it turned out, within a very short space of time I was back in my happy place writing a book – this time, one driven by my values. There is no doubt in my mind that I am where I am right now, writing down these words, because I took the time to do this work.

***

As we go through this exercise together now, remember that no one else ever needs to know your values unless you choose to tell them. You never need to explain or justify what is important to you – that it makes sense to *you* is all that matters. Engage with this exercise as if nobody is watching. Dance while you're at it, if you like. Having other people whispering their judgements and imperatives over your shoulder is not helpful at this stage (or any stage, actually). We want you to have the freedom and space to really connect back with yourself.

We hope that this feels like an exciting idea for you, but it may also feel scary. That's okay. Making new choices requires acting in the face of fear, not in the absence of it.

You may find that what matters most to you now connects all the way back to what has always mattered to you, but which has been obscured over the years by the many demands of life. Before we go on, cast your mind back to your childhood. What did you like doing then? What was important to you? If as a kid you really loved animals, you don't now have to retrain as a vet (although you could!) but having an animal in your life might be nourishing and important for you.

**ALICE.** When I was at school, I wanted to become an artist. It was a happy and creative place for me where my introversion could roam free and I could express myself without an audience. But I was given career advice by my school and told that artists don't earn a living, and anyway it wouldn't get me into a good university (no one thought to suggest art school . . .) so I dropped my art A-level in favour of something more 'academic'.

The values of 'success', 'academic achievement' and 'education' infused, even commanded, that decision and while they may not be my values *now*, I can radically accept that I was guided by them *then*. And it led me to a career in psychology, so no great harm. And art lingers somewhere on the periphery, occasionally coming into view and giving me happy hours of creation.

\*\*\*

Can you think of an equivalent? Families hold quite strong values, as do wider cultures. Girls not being educated well, or at all, for example, financial security, faith, independence – see if you can link your 'inherited' values to any of the big (and small) choices you have made.

Try to be honest with yourself. Notice how you judge what may or may not be important to you. Perhaps you feel embarrassed by one of your values, wishing it was something else instead. (As you saw, one of mine was abundance and I wondered if it made me seem greedy!) Don't listen to or trust these judgements, not for now, and maybe not ever. Hold them lightly, turn them down, mute them, bracket them. Whatever works.

## Breaking Free

An espalier is a frame used to train fruit trees to grow in a two-dimensional shape. Flat up against a wall or fence, their branches are forced to grow horizontally rather than upwards and outwards. But did anyone ask the tree what he, she, they thought? Despite such restrictions, the tree still grows on to fulfil its new destiny, but perhaps not the one it might have chosen for itself. Let's remove the shackles: your next chapter will be shaped *by* you, *for* you.

To help you to connect to your values now, here is a big list of possibilities. Read them through and notice which ones resonate with you. As you go through the list, try not to think too hard or dwell too long on anything at this stage, just note which ones chime. The list is not exhaustive. If you think of a value that's not on there, that's great too – add it on and choose it if you want. And don't worry about how many you go for – some people will choose a few and others nearly all of them! There is no right or wrong (that would be a judgement).

**Abundance** – to appreciate and invite in the fullness of life

**Acceptance** – to be open and accepting

**Accountability** – to own my actions

**Achievement** – to fulfil my goals

**Adventure** – to create, explore and seek novelty and stimulation

**Advocacy** – to speak up on behalf of others

**Assertive** – to respectfully stand up for my rights and needs

**Authenticity** – to be genuine and real, and true to myself

**Beauty** – to cultivate, create and nurture beauty in myself and all around me

**Care** – to look after myself and others

**Challenge** – to challenge myself to grow, learn and improve

**Charity** – to give and not to count the cost

**Commitment** – to follow through on my intentions

**Compassion** – to seek to understand and be kind

**Connection** – to foster relationships and community

**Contribution** – to make a positive difference

**Co-operation** – to be co-operative and collaborative

**Courage** – to persist in the face of fear

**Creativity** – to be innovative and expressive

**Fairness** – to treat people without discrimination

**Fitness** – to look after my physical and mental health

**Flexibility** – to adjust and adapt to changing circumstances

**Forgiveness** – to be forgiving towards myself and others

**Freedom** – to choose with autonomy and self-determination

**Friendliness** – to be friendly, companionable and agreeable

**Fun** – to seek out opportunities for fun

**Generosity** – to be generous, sharing and giving of myself

**Grace** – to act with dignity

**Gratitude** – to be grateful and appreciative

**Honesty** – to be truthful and open in all that I do

**Humour** – to find the funny

**Hope** – to believe in possibility

**Industry** – to be dedicated to the work I choose

**Integrity** – to honour my word

**Joy** – to delight in and be delighted by life

**Kindness** – to be considerate and nurturing

**Love** – to act lovingly and affectionately

**Mindfulness** – to be present to my experience

**Open-mindedness** – to be open to new ideas and perspectives

**Organisation** – to be orderly and efficient

**Passion** – to find and pursue what excites me

**Peace** – to be still and free from conflict

**Power** – to have confidence and influence over my life

**Safety** – to protect from physical or emotional harm

**Self-control** – to act with good judgement

**Sensuality** – to explore and enjoy my body

**Skilfulness** – to practise and improve my skills

**Spirituality** – to connect with something bigger than myself

**Trust** – to be honest and transparent

Once you have your list of values, the next step is to make them workable by grouping them together with others that are similar. For example, kindness and compassion might be in the same group. Take time with this, and it can be revisited as many times as you like over the coming days, weeks and months. For now, see if you can organise your values according to likeness into *four* groups.

Once you have your four groups, pick the value from each that best captures the spirit of the collective – one value word that will speak on behalf of all the others. You can also write the value definitions.

We hope that these values are starting to set your heart alight, just a little bit? They represent your new path ahead.

Imagine that you are on a boat in the Pacific, far out from the nearest land mass, with icy Alaska to the north and the warmer climes of Mexico to the east. You're longing to be on the beach, sipping mango juice and watching the sun set. You can't see land right now, so you need to set the direction of travel because you don't want to expend energy travelling towards the icy poles when you are hoping to reach a sunnier destination. Think of your values as your internal GPS, guiding you towards what is important to you even when storms rage, winds try to throw you off course and you can't see a damn thing.

Okay, let's put your GPS to the test.

Think now about a decision you need to make in the coming days. It could be something quite ordinary, like whether you're going to go out tonight, or it could be one of those bigger life decisions, such as whether to move house or change a relationship. Bring the upcoming decision to mind and note down all the possible choices you could make in relation to it.

With your GPS to hand, ask yourself this:
Which of these possible choices is most in service to my values?

The one that most aligns is the one that will take you towards yourself.

Let's say you are trying to work everything out and keep coming back to, 'I still love them.' Round and round you go, they have betrayed you, but you still love them – it's an impossible merry-go-round of a dialectic – *I love them and want to be with them and I want to leave them.* Now let's bring your values into focus and see if they can help guide your next choice. Let's say your values look like this:

*Integrity – to honour my word*
*Freedom – to choose with autonomy and self-determination*
*Grace – to act with dignity*
*Joy – to delight in and be delighted by life*

Which direction will take you towards a future aligned with what is important and meaningful to you and one which is led by integrity, freedom, grace or joy? If your values seem to contradict each other, for example, compassion takes you back to the one who's betrayed you, but freedom takes you in the other direction, be curious about that. It's a dialectic – hold the tension, because you can be both compassionate towards your betrayer and leave them. There will be times when you have to make decisions that take you off course – that's life – but overall, the weight of balance needs to be in favour of your values. It is through routinely asking yourself this question – *Is the decision I'm about to make in service to my values?* – that you'll create a future path aligned with what is most important to you.

Think of one action you could take today that would be fully aligned with one of your values. What is it?

Do it.

Choosing in this way is how you accumulate a meaningful and purposeful ongoing future. And you don't even have to ask yourself the question, 'What am I going to do with my future?', because your future is simply unfolding before your eyes with every single values-aligned decision you make.

## CHOICE POINTS

IN ANY GIVEN SITUATION WE HAVE A CHOICE . . . WE CAN MOVE
TOWARDS WHAT MATTERS TO US OR AWAY FROM IT

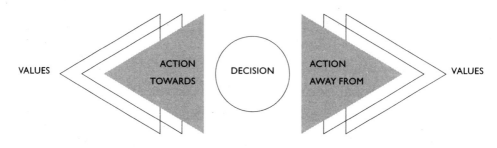

IS THE DECISION I'M ABOUT TO MAKE IN SERVICE TO MY VALUES?

When faced with a choice, you will find yourself pulled back in the direction of your old belief system, and this will take a while to change. The first thing to do when this happens is to take a moment to notice that you are doing it. Ask yourself, 'Am I using my fledgling belief to make this decision, or my flying belief?' Choose in the direction of your flying belief and your values, even if it feels a bit unusual, uncomfortable or peculiar. It won't feel this way for long.

Notice who in your life encourages you towards your values, who helps make effortless the manifestation of what matters to you – and notice who doesn't. If you find that your new values take you anywhere near a Dark Triad type, listen to your key people, remember the work you've done so far, and let them help steer you back on course.

## The Rickety Train

Imagine you are planning to take a train heading somewhere special that you've been longing to visit.[49]

You stand on the station platform, waiting for the train to arrive.

Two trains pull in, and you see that both are headed for your chosen destination.

One of them appears to be a bit dirty, shabby even, and you can see that some of the seats are worn and frayed. It looks odd, unfamiliar and uncomfortable.

The other one looks much safer, it's clean and the seats look really comfy and plush; it has free WIFI, air conditioning and a fancy dining car.

It feels risky to opt for the rickety train, so you hop aboard the safer-looking one and get settled.

Meanwhile, the rickety train pulls out of the station and makes its way towards your chosen destination. As you wait patiently you see another pull out, and then another.

Still – you think – it will be well worth the wait as surely the comfy train will leave soon.

But what if it never leaves the station?

What if the rickety train, despite looking shabby and uncomfortable is the only way to get to where you want to go?

Sometimes we get stuck in familiar grooves and turn away from the discomfort of the unknown, waiting for things to get better.

But here's the thing: if you keep making the same choices, the same things will keep happening. New choices do create discomfort, but might just take you where you're longing to get to.

# Chapter 17:

# New Perspectives

What do you see when you look at this picture?

Can you see the duck? And the rabbit? Over the previous pages you have created a new perspective on who you are, but that doesn't mean you will automatically lose sight of how you saw yourself before. As you move forward, expect some interplay, some movement back and forth between the different viewpoints – it's all part of the process of living into freedom. Much like this optical illusion where one picture can be seen in two ways, you can practise moving between views of yourself. And by being able to see both perspectives, you'll expand your view of yourself *and* your future.

Think of an elephant, a huge, fully grown elephant that has been tamed and put to work clearing forests. When it's not working, it is tied up with a chain attached to a peg in the ground to prevent its escape. With one stamp of its foot, the elephant could break free. But it doesn't. When it was young, it was tied up with the exact same chain, but wasn't big or strong enough to break it. As it grew, the imprint of that early experience endured, and even though as a grown adult one tug of its now mighty leg would be enough to break free – the elephant doesn't know this. The early lesson prevails, and the elephant's captivity is ensured. If only it knew . . .

The grown-up elephant doesn't know how to live freely, but you do.

Freedom is created the moment you realise you are not bound by your early beliefs, and that you can make different choices as an adult from the perspective of your flying beliefs. Living in that reality can feel both exhilarating and frightening.

There will be moments of uncertainty, even moments where you long for the familiarity and routine of your previous life, but if you just keep going, you will eventually see the full picture of your many possibilities.

When Irene was groomed by her betrayer for money, she blamed herself. She *knew* it was all her fault because, just like when she was young, she hadn't been careful and should have seen it coming. And so she resolved again to be more careful. But, armed with a new belief, she was able to have her elephant-stamping-its-foot moment. Her adult self told her young self what she was – capable, and full of fun and passion, and that she could trust herself. This was the pivotal moment for Irene. She saw the truth of it – her brother's accident wasn't her fault, and nor was the betrayal.

This was the new possibility she created:

*Irene*

*New perspective: I am capable and full of fun and passion. I can trust myself.*

*Values:*
*Adventure – to create, explore and seek novelty and stimulation.*

*Kindness – to be considerate and nurturing.*

*Fun – to seek out opportunities for fun.*

*Contribution – to make a positive difference.*

Nadia's perspective shifted from holding the fledgling belief: 'I am stupid and disappointing,' to a new, flying belief: 'I'm smart, and have a voice.' Once she realised that the strategy born of her fledgling belief hadn't spared her from being betrayed, she saw she no longer needed to hide away by asking so many questions, and so she created a new perspective.

This was the new possibility she created:

# Nadia

New perspective: I am smart and have a voice.

Values:

Industry – to be dedicated to the work I choose.

Passion – to find and pursue what excites me.

Abundance – to appreciate and invite in the fullness of life.

Courage – to persist in the face of fear.

Eshe's perspective shifted from the fledgling belief: 'I'm no good and it's my fault that bad things happen,' created when she fell and cut herself at her parents' barbecue, to a flying belief: 'I'm lovable, it's not my fault, I'm important and I can ask for help.' And with this shift, she no longer needed to keep everyone safe and put others first. And her own needs came into view.

This was the new possibility she created:

## Eshe

New perspective: I'm lovable. It's not my fault. I'm important and can ask for help.

Values:

Sensuality – to explore and enjoy my body.

Compassion – to seek to understand and be kind.

Fairness – to treat people without discrimination.

Mindfulness – to be present in my experience.

Lin's perspective shifted from her fledgling belief: 'I'm alone and no one will protect me,' to believing she possessed many new qualities to which she had previously been oblivious. When this came into view, she realised she could drop her old, 'win all the prizes' strategy and just be herself. Her new perspective was that she was 'cute, playful and kind'.

This was the new possibility she created:

# Lin

New perspective: I'm cute, resourceful, playful and kind.

Values:

Accountability – to own my actions.

Beauty – to cultivate, create and nurture beauty in myself and all around me.

Creativity – to be innovative and expressive.

Freedom – to choose with autonomy and self-determination.

Robyn saw that far from being 'alone and bad', she did matter, and her feelings did count, and with this she created and updated a new perspective that she was not only 'brave and good' but she was also 'precious and can be safe with others'. Instead of disconnecting to protect herself, she could connect with those around her.

This was the new possibility she created:

*Robyn*

*New perspective: I'm precious, and I can be safe with others.*

*Values:*

*Connection* – *to foster relationships and community.*

*Fitness* – *to look after my physical and mental health.*

*Joy* – *to delight in and be delighted by life.*

*Integrity* – *to honour my word.*

What is your new perspective? Bring to mind how your younger self felt in your memory, and how your adult self shifted that formative view. If you really believed that new perspective, if you really lived into your values, what might be possible for you now?

If you find yourself slipping back towards your fledgling beliefs and old protective strategies, don't judge yourself. Notice it's happening, be understanding and empathic towards yourself, and switch channels. Compassion is the antidote to judgement. You have worn the old jumper for such a long time, it's no wonder it's comfy and familiar. As you try on this new jumper, woven from your flying belief, it's going to take some getting used to. But trust us, once you've worn it in, this new jumper will become your firm favourite.

How does that feel? Sit with it for a bit . . .

If you now find that your old thoughts are flooding back, don't tell yourself not to think them, instead try this.

## Floating Leaves

Imagine it's a warm sunny day and you are sitting by a gentle meandering stream shaded by large oak trees.[50] The clear water flows over smooth rocks and pebbles as it descends through a peaceful valley.

Every so often, a big leaf drops from a branch and lands on the water in front of you.

As you watch this happen, start to become aware of your thoughts.

Each time a thought pops into your mind, imagine floating that thought out of your head and onto a leaf where you can watch it gently drifting past.

Don't try to make the stream go any faster or slower or try to change the thought on the leaf. Just let it be.

Enjoy this process, and don't worry if you become distracted or it feels hard, just gently turn your attention back to noticing your thoughts, placing them on the leaves and watching them float by.

# Chapter 18:

# The Court of Law

The time has come to rethink your story of heartbreak through the lens of everything you now know.

The betrayal dropped a bomb on your life story, spreading outwards from the epicentre and destroying not only your own relationship narrative but the wider ones in which it was embedded. It's as if you were halfway through reading a great book, only to find the rest of the pages ripped out and the bookshop where you bought it destroyed – along with your happy ending.

In your heart and mind you'd already written the whole story. Because our stories are so intimately connected with the people we love, when a significant relationship ends – and crucially here, not through our own choice – we struggle to reconcile what's happened with the story we always believed would play out. We were writing from a perspective that put our romantic relationship and our betrayal centre stage. A perspective that allowed our heartbreak to define us. How about we choose something different now? How about we pick up those ripped-out pages, stick them back in and carry on writing from a new perspective? You may not have chosen to be betrayed, but you can choose to be the author of what's next.

**RUTH.** I started my career as a lawyer, and practised for a decade as a criminal barrister. I was terrified about my first speech to the jury and convinced I'd done an awful job, that my terror had been glaringly obvious to everyone in court, and that the jury were bored. I entered the Bar robing rooms afterwards armoured up for criticism. The robing rooms are awash with backhanded banter, and I'm quite sure I gave as good as I got . . . 'That was a forensic speech' (inference: *it was boring and long-winded*); 'Lucky you, you've got such an easy case' (inference: *if you lose, you're a rubbish barrister*); 'I love the way you jumped around with your questions' (inference: *your cross-examination was all over the place*).

But my opponent made a point of congratulating me in the robing room. She was an older, seasoned barrister, and she told me how confident and convincing I'd sounded, commenting that I'd structured the speech well, starting with a powerful metaphor and finishing off with a pithy summary. She also told me that the jury were hanging on my every word. She may have been making it all up, of course, to be kind, having spotted my nerves. And while I continued to doubt her on the walk back home, I turned what she'd said over and over in my mind. I respected and admired her, so her comments were harder to dismiss, and because the specifics of what she said were also plausible (just about) and weren't compliments about how fabulous I looked in my wig and gown, I chose to accept her offering as another valid perspective on what had just happened.

She had given me something unexpected – a truthful compliment. I held what she'd said close to my chest and reminded myself of that 'jury hanging on my every word' comment whenever I was feeling nervous and every time before giving a speech. It never failed to give me a boost.

Have you ever had the experience of someone you respect recounting an experience in which you were the main character, but completely differently to your recollection of it? Perhaps they emphasised a strength you hadn't paid attention to, or a thoughtful response you didn't remember making, a power you hadn't valued?

This can go the other way, too. Negative feedback you didn't see coming can feel like a slap in the face. The dentist once told me at a routine check-up that I had receding gums and promptly sent a referral letter to a periodontist for gum graft surgery. Having never noticed my receding gums before he did, it was all I could see afterwards whenever I looked in the mirror. As it turns out, I reflected on what the dentist said and had the receding gums treated, and now have teeth I'd never even realised I wanted.

Do share the love by telling someone how you see them and helping them change their narrative of themselves, like that lovely barrister did for me. It can have a huge impact on their day, sometimes their whole life.

There are also perspectives about you that haven't even occurred to you yet. And there will be things other people see in you that can help shift how you see yourself, even when it might sound less than full of praise.

There are caveats to this. Not everyone can be trusted in their commentary. Be careful who you pay attention to and whose comments you take on board. A good question to ask yourself might be: does the person have any Dark Triad traits? Grant me the serenity to accept and the wisdom to spot Dark Triads – and always reject them out of hand! If their comments make you feel dismissed or helpless and desperate in any way, case dismissed. We all hurt each other sometimes and say regrettable things, because we are human, but it shouldn't routinely be the case. People you can trust will make you feel better or hopeful, even when what they have to say is challenging or critical.

And you still get to choose what comments to take on board. Always.

Another valuable lesson I learnt at the Bar was how much more power story has over facts. Whether defending or prosecuting a case, both sides receive identical witness statements, police reports, telephone transcripts, forensic evidence and photographs. Whichever side had instructed me, my job was to weave a story from that same bundle of evidence, a story which, by the end of the case – if I'd done a good-enough job – would bear no resemblance whatsoever to my opponent's.

My task was to rework the facts and material in such a way as to make a defendant *appear* innocent or guilty in the eyes of the jury. Take a robbery case, for example. The prosecution relied on the facts that a mobile phone had been stolen, a knife drawn, and my client had been identified by the victim. The question

I had to ask myself, representing the defendant, was how can I present the facts of the knife and the phone and my client having been identified to tell a different story, a story aligned with my client's case, a story powerful enough to persuade a jury to acquit them? What was the defendant doing with this alleged knife? Indeed, was there a knife at all or was it in fact a stainless-steel ruler? Wasn't it awfully dark at the time; how can you be sure it was them? Were they even there at all? Perhaps it was someone else? There was no phone; you are mistaken. You have a grudge against them and have made it all up. That kind of thing.

The key skill was always to try to use what had happened (the facts) to tell the story in a new and surprising way that had perhaps not occurred to anyone yet. And it was clear that at the Bar, as in life, a lack of facts had little bearing on how compelling a narrative you could weave. Indeed, if both barristers are any good, the jury often have the unenviable task of having to choose between two utterly different but equally compelling stories: one resulting in prison for the defendant, and the other, freedom.

***

Now for some fun . . .

You get to be the barrister for both sides. For and against. Pen and paper at the ready, please. Two columns. Write down the facts in defence of the fledgling belief in the first column. And only the facts (no conjecture, opinion or assumption). In the second column, list all the facts against it. Only the facts.

Let's hear from Nadia: Nadia's fledgling belief is that she is stupid. The facts in support of it are that she got the name of a bone wrong when she was six years old. The facts against it are that she got straight A's at school, holds a degree in sociology and is heading up a team at work.

Everything she had been telling herself in support of the fledgling belief was the story she had weaved on the back of it: everyone else is smarter than me; I never know the answers so have to ask all the questions; my fiancé is smarter than me; my dad is smarter than me. She was constantly comparing herself to others and finding herself falling short.

Now it's your turn. Do the facts add up to the story you've been telling yourself? Put yourself in the position of judge and jury. Who wins?

In our experience, a fledgling belief gets calcified by the story woven around it and has little to do with facts. Once you can divorce the facts from the story, what becomes clearer is that your fledgling belief was one of your earliest stories, one of the core narratives and so it's a sticky one, a very sticky one. But . . . the evidence you find to challenge it is in fact the seeds of a new story. So keep at it, keep gathering the evidence for the flying belief, keep weaving that new story, until it's as sticky as its predecessor. Sorry, what predecessor?

Deconstructing your own story in a court of law puts you back in charge of the narrative. Seeing yourself in your story from multiple different perspectives can help broaden and expand your sense of yourself, which brings other possible storylines into view. Your ability to rescript difficult material is a powerful weapon in your defence against the heartbreak.

Long after you've finished reading this book, you can revisit the idea of being a criminal barrister, rescript the case, and convict whatever sticky thought comes your way.

As you move forward, tuning into your new narrative is key. For now, think of your fledgling belief, and take a few minutes to write down any other beliefs about yourself that you may have formed around that time, within the context of your early nest. Now do the same for your flying belief, adding any other ones that occur to you about yourself. Now think of these two different accounts as two different radio channels. Give your fledgling belief's station a name, for example, 'Limiting FM' or 'Get Back in Your Box FM'. This is the prosecutor's voice, always finding fault and damning you. Now give the flying station a name, something uplifting, like 'EPIC FM'. Think of this station as your defence advocate and tune into it whenever you feel that fledgling belief and strategy coming back into play. This is the most important frequency to tune into. It is your wise adult empathic

mind, so turn up the volume when you get there.

Practise noticing when you are tuned into each channel and the difference in your experience when listening to each.

\*\*\*

With your wise and empathic adult mind at the helm, and the volume up high on EPIC FM, it's time to write another story.

You don't have to restrict yourself to the heartbreak story, unless you'd like to. Once again, length, style and tone are entirely up to you. You have a voice that is uniquely your own, which is infinitely more powerful than any other. What other people think has no place here. There is no right or wrong or better or worse way to do this, because only you can tell your story.

We'd like you to frame it around the following questions. When considering these questions, reflect on all the insights you've gained about yourself, your heartbreaker, your attachment patterns, bonding blueprints and the dynamics of your early nest. Keep your new perspectives close and your values GPS to hand and radically accept everything!

*What have you been through?*
*How have you coped?*
*What strategies have you used to keep yourself safe until now?*
*How are you going to move forward?*

# Chapter 19:

# Once Upon a Time

**Scene V**

**COSY DEN. NIGHT**

*In the den, the fire is roaring and all the women are seated. There is a connectedness within the group and the atmosphere is buoyant. Each of the women look different; furrowed brows appear relaxed, smiles have widened and deepened, eyes are twinkling; there is an aliveness to them and they comment among themselves on how fabulous they all look. ALICE tells them it's a thing – The Heartbreak Hotel Botox effect – and everybody laughs. IRENE, with one arm draped across the back of the sofa, says she feels as though her whole brain has been Botoxed. ROBYN appears focussed and refreshed. ESHE is smiling and at ease, both hands resting in her lap. LIN and NADIA occupy their seats*

*with a commanding presence, fully owning their space.*
*ALICE and RUTH turn towards LIN.*

LIN:     Okay, here goes. On his way to pick me up from gym-
         nastics, my father died in a car crash [*deep breath,*
         *coughing fit*]. My mother was left looking after the whole
         family and, as the eldest, I took on extra responsibili-
         ties because she was so busy, and although she put a
         brave face on it, I knew how sad she was. When her
         brother started coming over to help out, it cheered
         her up, it cheered us all up. But then he started to
         want to be alone with me, and that's when the rough
         and tumble became touching and stroking. I didn't tell
         anyone because I thought it was my fault, I thought
         it was a punishment for killing my dad, because if it
         wasn't for my gymnastics class, he'd still be alive. I was
         confused, and because I loved my uncle, and I loved
         my mother and they loved each other, and it seemed
         to make him happy, which made her happy, I never
         said a word. But I think she knew, how could she not,
         and that made me think it must be okay. But it wasn't.
         All these years I've blamed my mother and in my head
         I've had her in the dock over and over again [*tears*
         *rolling down her face*] and convicted her many times.
         Maybe when I grew up and left home I needed it to be
         her fault to make sense of how I'd allowed it to hap-
         pen, and to cope with the fact that it had happened. I
         don't know . . . But what I do know now is that it was not
         my fault.

*[Pause]*

And it was not my mother's fault either. It was my uncle's fault.

*[Pause]*

How have I coped? I coped by working hard and winning prizes to ward off the feeling that I was worth nothing. But no matter how well I did or how many times I won a medal or a prize, I never felt good enough. Nothing was ever enough to take away the empty and worthless feeling that I had as a child. And nobody cared anyway. I've been running and running yet somehow always ending up in the same place, exhausting myself in the process. And it's only now that I'm learning how to cope differently, that I've started to think I might be worth something after all. I am going to start taking better care of myself, just like I do for others . . . and leave those prizes behind.

*[Pause]*

I was led straight into the arms of Dickdust because he had won even more prizes than me, which I thought meant he must be a good person. He was ambitious and gorgeous and came from a good family that mine approved of. I was flattered by all the attention and overlooked many red flags. I met him after he gave a talk at the hospital about anaesthesia, and I remember that same evening a student nurse telling me that he was a cad, but I completely dismissed her and instead let myself become mesmerised by him. When he pulled my hair one night at a friend's engagement party and the next day laughed it off as a joke, I believed him, even though my intuition told me it was wrong. He was jealous and prone to violent outbursts and it was as unacceptable then as it is now, I just didn't see it at the time. There were lots of incidents like that, but I was so attracted to him, and believed so strongly that we were 'meant to be', with all those things we had in common and my family's enthusiasm, I was unable to see him for who he is. Because of everything I have learnt here, this is how I am going to move forward . . .

[*Pause*]

I will never fall for this sort of man again. Until I came here, I thought there was something wrong with me. I was good at my job but terrible in relationships, maybe it was even that because I was good at being a radiologist and so happy to be a doctor, there was a sort of justice to being unlucky in love. Because you can't have everything, can you? On some level, I believed that I deserved nothing more than what I got from Dickdust – crumbs of love and affection I begged for at his feet, like a starving dog. I have no experience of what safety looks like in a partner, but I'm determined to find out. I might create a spreadsheet or, who knows, develop an app or, at the very least, get potential partners to answer a questionnaire. Maybe Nadia can help me with that [LIN *winks at* NADIA, ALL *smile*]. Actually, there is a lovely man I knew from medical school who now works in paediatrics . . . he might not dazzle like Dickdust but maybe he's the safety I've been looking for. But first of all, I've got to get Dickdust out of the apartment [ALL *clap*]. Before this retreat I'd have married him if he'd asked me to, now I see I've dodged a bullet [ALL *cheer and laugh*].

*[Pause]*

All this time I've made excuses for him, even enabled his behaviour through my silence and submission, and all the while blamed myself, and my mother, when it is my uncle who is the one who should be in the dock, and Dickdust alongside him. My mother may not be perfect, but I know that she has her own demons to deal with and generations of expectation on her tiny shoulders too. Maybe she can come to The Heartbreak Hotel for the next retreat; everybody in my family should come and do this! Staying silent over all the things Dickdust has done and the things my uncle did has created a lot of shame. I've learnt that the only way to make this better is by speaking it out loud. Talking about what happened then and what is happening to me now is how I will reclaim power over my future and banish the shame. I've learnt from Robyn that doing one brave thing creates a ripple, and if we all stand up together in this way and call it out, we can make some serious waves and I've got enough on Dickdust to generate a tsunami.

[*Pause*]

When I get back home, I'm going to make two phone calls. The first to my mother. The second to the police. None of it was my fault, and I am not going to waste another minute of this precious life living as though it was. [*Smiles through tears;* ALL *are applauding*]

IRENE:   I've been ever so careful for so long now. Careful was how I ended up living in the same town I grew up in. Careful was how I married Stan – a man I was not even sexually attracted to. But he was the safe choice. Well, I thought he was, but now I see I was living in his shadow and the shadow he cast was long. He was careful too. Careful with me. Careful with money. Careful with his feelings. I don't want to do him down because he was a good man; he never got drunk, he never hit me, but . . . he liked me in my place, and he didn't like it when I stepped out of it or stood up for myself, and you know what, he did whatever he wanted, and went wherever he wanted and he was only able to build his business because of me. And that's the truth.

I'm thinking this should have all gone in my first story, but I guess I'm only being really honest with myself now. I've had a good life, never wanted for anything, so I thought his behaviour was a small price to pay. But now I see maybe it was a bit more expensive after all. I don't know. We were happy in our own way, but I understood happiness as being careful and safe. Careful was how I was as a mother, and careful didn't keep my sons close to me or to their sister. Far from it. They now live on opposite sides of the world. Maybe my being careful drove them away because they felt suffocated. Who knows? Careful didn't stop me from being betrayed either. Being careful did not keep me safe and it did not protect me from pain.

[*Pause*]

Now that I know how to turn down the volume on the old familiar radio station and tune into a new, much kinder, wiser one, which, by the way, is not at all careful and lives on a diet of radical acceptance, I see it very differently, and can tell my story in a new way . . .

[*Pause*]

Once upon a time there was a little girl who helped her mummy with her baby brother and was always cheerful. She loved climbing trees and running free and had a daring spirit. Her daddy was often away and this made her mummy sad, but the little girl kept thinking,

'If I try hard enough, I can cheer mummy up and she will be happy and everything will be okay.' And nothing made the little girl happier than making her mother laugh. Because she was such a good little girl, her mummy gave her bigger jobs: taking the baby to the park and making meals. The little girl loved this because she liked to pretend she was a mummy too and that her little brother was her own baby. It was all part of the adventure. The little girl wanted to cheer her mummy up on her birthday. She couldn't get her out of bed and the little girl didn't understand that it was because she was depressed and that it had nothing to do with her. Then the little girl nearly killed her baby brother with the boiling water from the kettle, and she decided that she was a bad girl after all. The little girl decided that the world was a dangerous place and that everything was scary and it was better to be careful and then everyone would be safe.

[*Pause*]

It didn't matter that she missed climbing trees and paddling in the stream, because the more careful she was, the fewer things went wrong. Being careful was working because her baby brother didn't get hurt again – even though his scarred face reminded the little girl each day how close he came to death – and her mummy did start talking to her again, eventually. The little girl missed her adventuring, but it seemed worth it to keep everyone safe, and so she gave up on her dream of becoming an explorer. The little girl decided a life of adventure was a very bad idea as accidents do happen, and to stop bad things from happening you have to be very, very careful.

[*Pause*]

The little girl grew up and didn't stray far from home, and she married the surest, safest boy from her school. As a big girl she tried very hard never to argue with her husband, but to swallow all his put-downs and always be careful – even with her feelings, and especially with her temper. She was so good at being careful that she forgot she even had one. She forgot she had feelings at all. When her husband died, she was careful in her grief, careful not to let it show in case she upset her grown-up children. She was careful and she was lonely. And because she didn't believe in herself and hadn't had much of a sex life, when Lucifer came along, she was flattered by all the attention and let her guard down. Because she loved him she would have done anything for him, so she gave him money for his brother. She was furious when she found out she'd been played, because she had been so careful and couldn't understand that such a bad thing had happened to such a careful person ... until she went back in time and met up with the young girl she once was, standing next to her burning brother with the kettle at his feet, and took hold of her little hand and told her that it was not her fault – that none of it was her fault [*voice shaky, tears welling*].

[*Pause*]

The truth is, this insight has only been made possible because of my betrayal. He can have the money. I have my freedom now. I might be too old to climb trees, but then again . . . [*Whoops from* ALL]

[*Pause*]

The good thing about having been so careful is that Stan and I were careful with money too, and he made quite a bit of it. So even though Lucifer stole a lot, I've no mortgage to pay and more than enough to live off – if I'm careful . . . only joking! I'm never using that word again. Instead of a swear jar, I'm going to have a 'careful' jar and if I ever do anything 'careful', or use the word at all, I'll put a pound into that jar and use all the money to do something seriously bloody un-careful. I'm done with it. I've always been drawn to India, but never allowed myself to follow up on it, because of course, there's nothing careful about travelling to the Himalayas to go trekking [*cheering*]. My friend Claire might even fancy joining me, and I'm going to ask her as soon as I get home [NADIA *wolf whistles*].

[*Pause*]

I'm going on an adventure. I gave up on all that because of an accident that had nothing to do with me. So . . . it's first stop India, and then on to my grandchildren in Australia, where I'm going to take them to do something daring and wild. My sons won't recognise me. I've not got it all planned out either, because I trust now that it's all going to be okay, that I'm going to be okay. We're all going to be okay.

[ALL *clap*. ALICE *looks to* NADIA *and nods*]

NADIA:   Looking back, I know I was lucky to have such good parents and no siblings, especially after hearing what you lot had to put up with – no offence [*wry smile*]. But I also think that because they are good people and so accepting about my sexuality, I glossed over the fact that there was other stuff going on that restricted me from developing fully. I never would have thought that asking lots of questions could be a problem, but I see now that I've worn my questions like a shield to defend against anyone getting to really know me and finding out that I'm stupid. And I wasn't always tuned in to the answers, which often rebounded off me because it wasn't curiosity driving them, but fear. I asked questions so I would stay hidden and I now see that this is why I have struggled to make close connections. People liked me because my questions made them feel special and Frosty was attracted to me because I seemed so interested in everything she said and did. And I think it made her feel important which I guess was her stuff, having come from a chaotic home where she was largely ignored. My questions gave her what she didn't get growing up – a feeling of being valued. But once the honeymoon period wore off, she stopped being interested in me, and neither of us could recapture that initial chemistry. We were a typical Lone and Close Ranger pairing. After the intensity wore off, she started retreating whenever I came near, and the more I tried to find her and draw her back to me, the further away she went. As time marched on, we went off key and couldn't get back in tune no matter how hard we tried.

[*Pause*]

I don't feel good about what happened. I am still heartbroken, and I don't want to forgive her for what she did – and I'm glad you never asked me to because I don't and I won't. But what I can do is accept my part in the breakdown of our relationship. Because of my difficulties with communicating freely and openly, and my fear of being seen as stupid, and therefore rejected, I couldn't really cope when things started to go wrong. I became desperate for her attention rather than accepting that maybe she just needed some space. So I'm grateful I got clear about that because I know exactly what's needed now to move forward and how to create a good relationship with a future wife. My values will steer me on the right course. Industry is going to propel me forward in my career, which has stagnated because I have been afraid. Passion is what's going to inspire me and through letting it lead me I'll get to know what really makes me tick. Next is courage – to go for things, even though I might be afraid. And my fourth value is to manifest the spirit of abundance because I want to live a life that's full to the brim.

[*Pause*]

I was a lonely little girl and I've never admitted that to myself or to my family. I spent a lot of time reading and playing on my own in my bedroom. It was my safe place, my happy place. And it still can be my happy place so long as I'm also able to be with others in a real and honest way and not hide myself from everyone. I have another voice that's not always quiet and questioning, which has been hidden behind the curtain of long-ago beliefs created by a six-year-old who didn't want to be humiliated by not knowing the answer ever again. This other voice is clear and sure of itself, if a little out of practice. So . . . that's me. I am capable and smart and I have a voice.

ALICE:   You are and you do, Nadia. Now, Robyn, we're so glad you're still here and didn't leave yesterday. Are you ready?

ROBYN:  Yes I am. And thank you, Alice and Ruth, for not kicking me out. My God, yesterday feels like a thousand
years ago now. I'm so glad I stayed. Now that I have my
values-GPS steering me right, I will celebrate connection in all my relationships. Cherish my physical and
mental health. Find joy in the everyday. Live a life of integrity and honour my word. Those are my values and
I love them all!

[*Pause*]

The biggest one for me is connection. I want to recon-
nect with my daughters. I now see their low opinion
of me is a result of my addiction, but the addiction is
not who I am, it is how I have coped. I'm going to have
compassion for myself and not beat myself up about
it any longer. I will ask for their forgiveness, and I will
forgive myself. I will own up to what's been going on for
me and rejoin Alcoholics Anonymous, and take each
day as it comes. This time it will be different because I
have you good women to keep me straight and I have
all this knowledge and wisdom that has come from doing this work. When I wake up with the jitters at 3 a.m.,
Lin will be in the middle of the afternoon and might
be on a break, and Eshe will be making the little one's
breakfast. What I mean is, whatever state we are in, at
whatever time of day or night, all of us are only ever
one text message away from each other. That is such a
wonderful thought, isn't it? What a gift.

[*Pause*]

I failed with AA before because my fledgling beliefs were that everything's unfair and everyone hates me and I'm ridiculous and my feelings are irrelevant. To cope with all this, I shut myself away from everybody, I shut myself down. I thought that in doing this I wouldn't be blamed or hurt, but instead when I cut off from everybody I got blamed anyway and I hurt myself and my daughters through my drinking. You heard it here first.

As you know, my husband and I built a home together in South West France to retire to. But, if I'm being honest, I was only ever half there throughout the marriage. The drinking started after our first daughter. I had postnatal depression and was self-medicating – although that is no excuse. I was afraid to ask for help. I always thought I was independent, but I was actually co-dependent and my partner in crime was the alcohol, and my girls deserve better than that. I deserve better too. I know that I grew up in a dodgy nest but I'm not going to let that define me anymore. Yes my brother was a bully, but he had a hard time too. I can see that now.

[*Pause*]

As for Voldemort, the sad truth is that, yes, he has left me for a more soulful love; God, his mid-life crisis is such a cliché. But I was disconnected a lot of the time, and because of that I wasn't able to be intimate with him. All his requests for a cuddle were met with me running for the hills, often with a bottle of vodka in my back pocket. He has been horrible to me, and I don't excuse him any of his behaviour. To leave me so soon after my diagnosis is callous and cruel. However, I do feel that my greatest betrayal has come from me – against myself. And bringing that into the light is what's going to save me. Not reconciling with an arsehole who left me when I needed him most. I want to end my story by saying something to Lin. [ROBYN *turns towards* LIN, *who puts her hand on her heart and smiles*]

[*Pause*]

I came back because of you. When you told us about your uncle, I remembered my own abuse, something that I'd buried so deep and for so long, I had almost forgotten it happened. I'd inebriated myself against it rising up to the surface. I was terrified of the feelings that came with the awful memories, so I got in my car and left. But then I thought of you and I didn't want you to feel shame in having bravely shared what had happened to you or to think I couldn't handle hearing it – and so I came back. Because of all of you here, when I got back to my room, I didn't have a drink.

[ROBYN *reaches into her bag, pulls out an unopened gin bottle and places it on the table, hands shaking*]

Because of you, I told my story too. Thank you, Lin, for the gift of you, for the gift of sharing your story. Your vulnerability became my courage.

[LIN *stands, goes to* ROBYN, *big hug. When everyone is settled again,* ALICE *turns to* ESHE]

ESHE:   Robyn, I've got so much from you this weekend. Both my parents drank; they worked long hours in gruelling jobs and I was left in charge a lot. Because of the drinking, they were often absent or angry for no reason, which is why I had to be so vigilant all the time and was too scared to ask them for help. I see now that my anxiety stemmed from my upbringing, which was busy and chaotic with everybody battling for Mum's attention.

[*Pause*]

When Robyn talked about her daughters not trusting her and blaming them, it really reminded me of my own parents; it's exactly what they did – blamed me for things going wrong, things that were their responsibility, not mine. So thank you, Robyn, for admitting to being an alcoholic so I could realise my own parents were too [*a nod between* ESHE *and* ROBYN]. And I don't blame them, or anyone else for that matter. My dad thought his anger issues were nothing compared to his own father's, who once broke his arm with a branch he'd snapped off a tree. He told us this story to legitimise the violence he used against us. He never used a stick or a belt or a shoe; we didn't know how easy we had it, he'd say . . . that sort of thing. God only knows what his father's parents were like but I'm going to take a wild guess and say they probably weren't the best, and not blame them either. Because what's the point? My dad's drinking got worse after Mum died and he became more and more distant from us and from himself. I see now this is an exact mirror of my husband's behaviour in our marriage and that none of it is my fault.

[*Pause*]

I was constantly fluffing up Ballsack – that sounds so wrong!

[*Giggles from* ALL]

I did everything I could to please him, but it was never going to be enough, which meant it could never be right between us. He'll never be right for anyone, because they won't satisfy him either. No one can. I hate the phrase sex addiction – it sounds like an excuse men invented for themselves to get away with their sexual greed, but maybe there is something in it. We were having sex and the whole time he was at it online and offline with these other women. Even if we'd had sex twice a day, he'd have still found time to betray me. Despite all this I can't remember ever feeling so free as I do right now in this very moment.

[*Pause*]

There wasn't much talk of feelings where I grew up. Everybody was too busy trying to survive. But my feelings have been there all along, even if they never had a name or a time or a place to just be, it didn't mean they weren't there. I tried to get away from them because I lived in fear of them controlling me. But I don't have to live like that anymore. Just learning to let the feelings come knowing that they will pass has been a revelation. After this weekend, I am going to trust them more and listen to what else my anger might be telling me.

[*Pause*]

I am a Roller Ranger, but nothing is going to overwhelm me. I know that now. If I notice myself struggling against what's happening, I'll get out my Chinese Finger Trap to remind myself how to let go. So thank you for showing me the way, and for being the green that I so badly needed. When I came on this retreat I thought I still loved Ballsack, and that I couldn't raise our children on my own. I was hoping to find the strength to forgive him and to allow him to come back to us. But now I see how far away from myself I had travelled, and in this journey alongside all you amazing women

I have finally arrived – not where I imagined, but back home. Back home with myself. My heart may have been broken, but I'm no longer ruminating on why he was so sweet on me once and how it all went sour. Now, released from the chains of self-blame, I can feel my spirit growing strong again. I will rise from the ashes of my loss and my children will rise with me. Because if I am not afraid to stride out on my own and build something new, they won't be afraid to follow. I know who I am now and maybe that's all any of us ever really need to know. My name is Eshe and I matter.

ALICE:   Reader, are you ready to share your story with us?

# Chapter 20:

# Daring to Choose

Forest fires burn away undergrowth that prevents sunlight reaching the forest floor – sunlight that enables new plants to grow on the ashes of the old. Fire is the disruptor that drives growth, giving both plant and animal species new opportunities to grow strong. It turns out that even something as devastating as a forest fire makes a vital contribution to the health of the forest.

Your heartbreak is that forest fire, and from the ashes of your loss seeds of new growth have taken root. To grow that precious seed of hope within you, accept that the fire has happened. Day after day, hour after hour, minute after minute, choose to accept – radically – that your heart has been broken. It was not your choice and you can't change that it happened, but you do have choices now. And it is these choices that can turn the scorched landscape of your soul into the birthplace of your hope.

Which scenarios and choices are you struggling with at the moment? We invite you to write them down and then place them on a continuum, with those you have the least control over at one end and those you have the most control over at the other. Here are some examples from your fellow guests.

*They never pick up the kids on time.*

*Are they going to make me move out of the house?*

*Will they come back to me?*

*Am I going to file for divorce?*

*Do they still love me?*

If any of your scenarios fall towards the 'no control' end of the continuum, let go of the rope. And for those scenarios and choices that you *can* do something about, write down some different courses of action you could take. Once you have two or three feasible options, we invite you to choose the one most aligned with your values and take the first step towards making it happen.

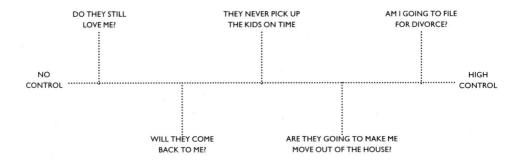

There is another choice that frames everything that is happening around you: the meaning you give it. From the moment we are born, our task is to make meaning from our experience against a backdrop of uncertainty that there is any meaning at all. We imbue our experience with significance so that we can anchor ourselves and create a degree of coherence and predictability in our lives. 'Why are we here?' is perhaps the biggest existential question of all, and no one has yet found a universally satisfactory answer. For some, we are fulfilling the will of God, for others we are slowly making our way along the evolutionary chain. Without any universal truth, we are responsible for creating our own sense of meaning throughout our lives. And meaning is not just a response to our experience – meaning creates our experience.

Remember the perspective picture, where you could see both the duck and the rabbit? This is your mind's capacity to attribute different meaning to the same image, reflected in the perspective you choose to adopt.

If your heartbreaker was unfaithful, here are some meaning-choices you could make:

*They were a sex addict.*

*They were a narcissist who sought only their own pleasure.*

*I'm unlovable.*

*They left because I'm not attractive enough.*

*The world is an unfair place, and wonderful women get betrayed.*

*It shouldn't have happened – my life is over.*

And it's not just for the big stuff – we make meaning-choices about our everyday difficulties too. Let's say your heartbreaker isn't returning your calls. You could choose to attach any one of these different meanings to that fact (and feel free to add your own):

*They didn't get the message.*

*I am ugly/fat/stupid.*

*They hate me.*

*They are punishing me.*

*I am irrelevant.*

*They are in bed with their lover.*

*I am unlovable.*

*They are a narcissistic twat.*

The meaning you make affects the feelings you have about what happened. And the meaning is yours to choose. Always.

# Chapter 21:

# A Mighty Wind

The smallest action you take now can have great significance on your life in ways you might never imagine. Chaos theory teaches us that the outcome of any process, though sensitive to its starting point, may bear no resemblance to it. A butterfly flaps its wings in Brazil and the tiny amount of air pressure it exerts causes a typhoon in Texas.

This is what's possible for you – and for all women. What you do next counts. What we all do next counts – in all kinds of unforeseen ways. You may not see a clear pathway forward just yet. Sometimes you will find yourself in a dense fog and all you can see is what's right in front of you, and that's okay, because all you ever need is your next move. And if you lead from your flying belief, you're heading towards hope; if you lead with compassion and courage, you're heading towards confidence; if you lead with your values, you are heading towards purpose and joy. You have dared to explore who you are, you have dared to connect to your deepest vulnerabilities, and you have dared to choose to let go. Knowledge may be power, but insight is alchemy.

Keep that photo of your younger self near. Look after her, remember her dreams and tend to her needs. Sweep away any shameful beliefs she held, because they weren't meant for her and they are not meant for you. You deserve kindness and respect and love and so does she. Refusing to be diminished by those around you is an act of resistance – you are not less than anyone else and you are more than you ever imagined.

You don't need to do this alone. When women connect with one another in deep empathy and sit in silence as each speaks her truth, this act of unity and love sends out a powerful message – that we all stand together. This is how we build each other up. When you are in pain, remember others are too. Connect with them. Coming together and sharing our vulnerabilities is how we join the dots of our experience and link hands with one another. Find your people. It is your community that will carry you. As you move forward, take what you have learnt, advocate for it – amplify it – because it is relevant to everyone. Link up with others and lean out. Love wisely, stand up for each other, and share your stories.

Our hope for you is that you choose to think and act in ways that build you up. That you take responsibility only for what you can control. That you take the definitions others give you with a pinch of salt if they make you feel any less of a woman. That you act in service to your values. That you take the time you need – less than you imagine, but more than you will want to give. That you let go of the rope, or don't pick it up at all. That you keep yourself cosy, have a good laugh when you can, and always take that nap.

You have what you need now, so keep making your next move, and before you know it, you'll be somewhere you never thought you'd be. It's not for us to know where that is. But we do know that you have many possibilities, and it is within these that your hope lies.

Imagine this . . .

All the strength and all the vulnerability of all the women all over the world circulating like starlings in the sky, in perfect unison and beautiful formation. Think of the air pressure it would create – nothing would ever be the same again. The power generated would raise from the ground all those on their knees, and show them how much they matter, just as you do.

Spread your wings . . . a mighty wind is coming.

# Postscript

NADIA was promoted to head of HR for a global organisation and relocated to New York, where she has set up home with her gorgeous kitten, Cookie. She is enjoying answering more questions than she's asking.

IRENE's latest update on the WhatsApp group was a photo she posted of herself white-water rafting down the Zambezi.

ESHE is studying for a PhD alongside her senior lectureship. At weekends, she volunteers at the domestic violence shelter with her eldest daughter.

ROBYN's unmentionable is living in France with the mosaic tile man he met in Santorini. She is reconnecting with her daughters and still hasn't had a drink . . .

LIN is dating the paediatrician. She doesn't know it yet, but tonight when he takes her for a birthday supper, he's going to propose. In case you are worried about his attachment pedigree, he is a Safe Harbour. Her mother is going to be their best woman.

As for you . . . do let us know.

# Notes

**Introduction**

1. Kristina Coop Gordon, Donald H. Baucom, and Douglas K. Snyder, 'An Integrative Intervention for Promoting Recovery from Extramarital Affairs', *Journal of Marital and Family Therapy* 30, no. 2 (April 2004): 213–31, https://doi.org/10.1111/j.1752-0606.2004.tb01235.x

2. Michael Linden, 'Posttraumatic Embitterment Disorder', *Psychotherapy and Psychosomatics* 72, no. 4 (July–August 2003): 195–202, https://doi.org/10.1159/000070783.

3. N. Padmavathi, T. S. Sunitha, and G. Jothimani, 'Post Infidelity Stress Disorder', *Indian Journal of Psychiatric Nursing* 5, no. 1 (2013): 56–59, https://doi.org/10.4103/2231-1505.261777.

4. Victoria Williamson, Dominic Murphy, Andrea Phelps, David Forbes, and Neil Greenberg, 'Moral Injury: The Effect on Mental Health and Implications for Treatment', *The Lancet Psychiatry* 8, no. 6 (2021): 453–55.

5. Timothy R. Levine, *Duped: Truth-Default Theory and the Social Science of Lying and Deception* (Tuscaloosa: Univ. Alabama Press, 2020).

6. Rowena Pagdin, Paul M. Salkovskis, Falguni Nathwani, Megan Wilkinson-Tough, and Emma Warnock-Parkes, ' "I Was Treated like Dirt": Evaluating Links between Betrayal and Mental Contamination in Clinical Samples', *Behavioural and Cognitive Psychotherapy* 49, no. 1 (2021): 21–34, https://doi.org/10.1017/S1352465820000387.

7. Brian D. Earp, Olga A. Wudarczyk, Bennett Foddy, and Julian Savulescu1, 'Addicted to Love: What Is Love Addiction and When Should It Be Treated?', *Philosophy, Psychiatry, Psychology* 24, no. 1 (March 2017): 77–92, https://doi.org/10.1353/ppp.2017.0011.

8. Dean Takahashi, 'Ashley Madison: Affairs in the Time of Coronavirus', *Venture Beat*, March 28, 2020, https://venturebeat.com/2020/03/28/ashley-madison-affairs-in-the-time-of-coronavirus/.

9. Sebastian, 'Ashley Madison User, Growth and Cheating Statistics (2022)', RelationshipAdvice.co, last modified August 11, 2023, https://relationshipsadvice.co/ashley-madison-statistics/.

10. Kristina Coop Gordon and Erica A. Mitchell, 'Infidelity in the Time of COVID-19', *Family Process* 59, no. 3 (September 2020): 956–66, https://doi.org/10.1111/famp.12576.

11. Benjamin Warach and Lawrence Josephs, 'The Aftershocks of Infidelity: A Review of Infidelity-Based Attachment Trauma', *Sexual and Relationship Therapy* 36, no. 1 (2019): 68–90, https://doi.org/10.1080/14681994.2019.1577961.

12. Howard E. LeWine, 'Broken-Heart Syndrome (Takotsubo Cardiomyopathy)', Harvard Health Publishing: Harvard Medical School, June 13, 2023, https://www.health.harvard.edu/heart-health/takotsubo-cardiomyopathy-broken-heart-syndrome.

13. Communications Team, 'First Treatment for "Broken Heart Syndrome" Trialled', University of Aberdeen, June 29, 2022, https://www.abdn.ac.uk/news/16140/.

14. Howard E. LeWine, 'Broken-heart Syndrome (takotsubo cardiomyopathy)', *Harvard Health Publishing* (June 2023): https://www.health.harvard.edu/heart-health/takotsubo-cardiomyopathy-broken-heart-syndrome

15. Sandeep M. Patel, et al., 'Distinctive clinical characteristics according to age and gender in apical ballooning syndrome (takotsubo/stress cardiomyopathy): an analysis focusing on men and young women', *Journal of Cardiac Failure* 19, no. 5 (2013): 306–10. doi:10.1016/j.cardfail.2013.03.007

16. Victoria L. Cammann, Konrad A. Szawan, Barbara E. Stähli, Ken Kato, et al., 'Age-Related Variations in Takotsubo Syndrome', *Journal of the American College of Cardiology* 75, no. 16 (2020): 1896–77, https://doi.org/10.1016/j.jacc.2020.02.057.

17. J. Lee, A. Wachholtz, KH. Choi, 'A Review of the Korean Cultural Syndrome Hwa-Byung: Suggestions for Theory and Intervention', *Asia Taepyongyang Sangdam Yongu.* (January 2014): https://doi:10.18401/2014.

18. Sara Wallström, Kerstin Ulin, Sylvia Määttä, Elmir Omerovic, Inger Ekman, 'Impact of Long-Term Stress in Takotsubo Syndrome: Experience of Patients', *European Journal of Cardiovascular Nursing* 15, no. 7 (December 2016): 522–28, https://doi.org/10.1177/1474515115618568.

**Chapter 2: Your Story**

19. Stephen J. Lepore, Melanie A. Greenberg, Michelle Bruno, Joshua M.Smyth, 'Expressive Writing and Health: Self-Regulation of Emotion-Related experience, Physiology, and Behaviour', in *The Writing Cure: How Expressive Writing Promotes Health and Emotional Well-Being*, eds. Stephen J. Lepore and Joshua M. Smyth, (Washington, DC, American Psychological Association, 2002), 99–117, https://doi.org/10.1037/10451–005.

20. Deborah Siegel-Acevedo, 'Writing Can Help Us Heal from Trauma', *Harvard Business Review*, published July 1, 2021, https://hbr.org/2021/07/writing-can-help-us-heal-from-trauma.

21. Joanne Frattaroli, 'Experimental Disclosure and Its Moderators: A Meta-Analysis', *Psychological Bulletin* 132, no. 6 (2006), 823–65, https://doi.org/10.1037/0033-2909.132.6.823.

22. The Dropping Anchor metaphor is adapted from Russ Harris, *The Happiness Trap: How to Stop Struggling and Start Living* (Umhlanga Rocks, South Africa: Trumpeter Books, 2008).

**Chapter 4: Rumination**

23. Namiko Kamijo and Shintaro Yukawa, 'The Role of Rumination and Negative Affect in Meaning Making Following Stressful Experiences in a Japanese Sample', *Frontiers in Psychology* 9 (November 2018): 2404, https://doi.org/10.3389/fpsyg.2015.01335.

24. Samantha M. Jones and Erin A. Heerey, 'Co-Rumination in Social Networks. Emerging Adulthood', *Emerging Adulthood* 10, no. 6 (2022), 1345–60, https://doi.org/10.1177/21676968221111316.

25. A. Borders, 'Ruminations and Related Constructs: Causes, Consequences, and Treatment of Thinking Too Much', (2020), Academic Press.

26. Thomas F. Denson, "The Multiple Systems Model of Angry Rumination," *Personality and Social Psychology Review* 17, no. 2 (2013), 103–23, https://doi.org/10.1177/1088868312467086.

27. Thomas F. Denson, "The Multiple Systems Model of Angry Rumination," *Personality and Social Psychology Review* 17, no. 2 (2013), 103–23, https://doi.org/10.1177/1088868312467086.

28. The Tiger Cub metaphor is adapted from Steven C. Hayes, *Get Out of Your Mind and Into Your Life: The New Acceptance and Commitment Therapy* (Oakland, CA: New Harbinger Publications, 2005).

29. The Chinese Finger Trap metaphor is adapted from Steven C. Hayes, *Get Out of Your Mind and Into Your Life: The New Acceptance and Commitment Therapy* (Oakland, CA: New Harbinger Publications, 2005).

### Chapter 5: Scene II

30. Adapted from Paul McKenna, *Instant Influence and Charisma: Master the Art of Natural Charm and Ethical Persuasiveness* (London: Bantam, 2015).

### Chapter 6: Radical Acceptance

31. Jeffrey Brantley, Jeffrey C. Wood, and Matthew McKay, *The Dialectical Behavior Therapy Skills Workbook* (Oakland, CA: New Harbinger, 2007).

32. The Troll and the Hole metaphor is adapted from Steven C. Hayes, *Get Out of Your Mind and Into Your Life: The New Acceptance and Commitment Therapy* (Oakland, CA: New Harbinger Publications, 2005).

### Chapter 8: Bonding Blueprints

33. Kelly-Ann Allen, Margaret L. Kern, Christopher S. Rozek, Dennis M. McInerney & George M. Slavich 'Belonging: a review of conceptual issues, an integrative framework, and directions for future research', *Australian Journal of Psychology*, (2021) 73:1, 87–102, https://doi.org/10.1080/00049530.2021.1883409

34. Jill Sakai, 'How Synaptic Pruning Shapes Neural Wiring during Development and, Possibly, in Disease', *PNAS* 17, no. 28: 16096–99, https://doi.org/10.1073/pnas.2010281117.

35. Harry F. Harlow, Margaret Harlow, 'Learning to Love', *American Scientist* 54, no. 3 (1966): 244–72. http://www.jstor.org/stable/27836477.

36. John Bowlby, *Attachment*, 2nd ed. (New York: Basic Books, 1982).

37. This term corresponds to the more commonly used secure attachment style.

38. This term corresponds to the more commonly used avoidant attachment style.

39. This term corresponds to the more commonly used anxious attachment style.

40. This term corresponds to the more commonly used disorganised attachment style.

41. Jeffry A. Simpson and W. Steven Rholes, 'Adult Attachment, Stress, and Romantic Relationships', *Current Opinion in Psychology* 13 (February 2017): 19–24, https://doi.org/10.1016/j. copsyc.2016.04.006.

### Chapter 9: The Dark Triad

42. Monica A. Koehn, Ceylan Okan, and Peter K. Jonason, 'A Primer on the Dark Triad Traits', *Australian Journal of Psychology* 71, no. 1 (2019): 7–15, https://doi.org/10.1111/ajpy.12198.

43. Lawrence, Josephs, 'Fatal Attractions: The Dark Triad and Infidelity', in *The Dynamics of Infidelity: Applying Relationship Science to Psychotherapy Practice* (Washington, DC: American Psychological Association, 2018), 89–111, https://doi.org/10.1037/0000053-005.

44. Grant Hilary Brenner, '11 Ways People Try to Hide Their Infidelity: 5. Use Friends for Coverage', *Psychology Today*, published January 9, 2022, https://www.psychologytoday.com/gb/blog/experimentations/202201/the-top-11-ways-people-try-hide-infidelity.

45. Timothy R. Levine, *Duped: Truth-Default Theory and the Social Science of Lying and Deception* (Tuscaloosa: Univ. Alabama Press, 2020).

**Chapter 13: Power and Shame**

46. Joanne L. Bagshaw, *The Feminist Handbook* (Oakland, CA: New Harbinger, 2019).

**Chapter 15: Emotional Regulation**

47. Adapted from Paul Gilbert, *The Compassionate Mind* (London: Constable, 2010).

48. I. Jarero and L. Artigas, 'The EMDR Integrative Group Treatment Protocol: EDMR Group Treatment for Early Intervention following Critical Incidents', *European Review of Applied Psychology* 62, no. 4 (October 2012): 219–22, https://doi.org/10.1016/j.erap.2012.04.004.

**Chapter 16: The Compass**

49. The Rickety Train metaphor is adapted from Jill A. Stoddard and Niloofar Afari, *The Big Book of ACT Metaphors: A Practitioner's Guide to Experiential Exercises and Metaphors in Acceptance and Commitment Therapy* (Oakland, CA: New Harbinger Publications, 2014).

**Chapter 17: New Perspectives**

50. The Floating Leaves metaphor is adapted from Jill A. Stoddard and Niloofar Afari, *The Big Book of ACT Metaphors: A Practitioner's Guide to Experiential Exercises and Metaphors in Acceptance and Commitment Therapy* (Oakland, CA: New Harbinger Publications, 2014).

# Acknowledgements

Special thanks . . .

To our number one champion and a stellar agent, Chandler Crawford, and the team at Transatlantic Literary Agency for launching our book into the world.

To our forensic and sensitive editors on both sides of the pond – Elizabeth Mitchell and Louise McKeever – and to our phenomenal publisher, Lisa Milton, for stewarding us through the entire process and for being, well, one of the most epic women to walk the earth.

Thanks to the powerhouse that is Cathryn Summerhayes, our brilliant agent, and everyone involved at Curtis Brown.

To assistant editor Ghjulia Romiti, copyeditor Shari Black and proofreader Helena Caldon for doing such an eagle-eyed job of polishing the manuscript. To Maria Nilsson for the beautiful illustrations, Rosamund Saunders for the interior design and to Stephanie Heathcote for the front cover.

To our friends and champions from far and wide, for the listening and advising and endless support and cheerleading.

To our families, in particular, Jean-Paul, Sonny, Isla, Olly, Rufus and Sebastian – for facilitating writing trips, never losing faith and inspiring us in all manner of ways.

To each other – for all the hard thinking and endless rewrites, for spurring each other on when we didn't think we had anything left in the tank, and for still making each other laugh, even when another little darling was up for the chop.

To all our women from all around the world who have connected with us at The Heartbreak Hotel and who have come on retreat. You're the reason we're all here. Keep on shining, so others can too.

**Alice Haddon** and **Ruth Field** have been friends for thirty years, sharing their stories and supporting each other through their many heartbreaks. Alice is a counselling psychologist with twenty-five years' experience in both public and private psychology services. She also works as an academic and lecturer at City, University of London. Ruth is an accredited coach and motivational self-help author with a masters degree in Creative Writing. She spent a decade working as a criminal barrister. Both women are passionate advocates for women's mental health. Alice is an associate fellow of the British Psychological Society and a Health and Care Professionals Council registered practitioner psychologist. Ruth is a member of the Criminal Bar Association, the Association for Coaching, and the International Society for Coaching Psychology.

HQ
An imprint of HarperCollins*Publishers* Ltd
1 London Bridge Street
London SE1 9GF

www.harpercollins.co.uk

HarperCollins Publishers
Macken House, 39/40 Mayor Street Upper,
Dublin 1, Ireland, D01 C9W8

1

First published in Great Britain by
HQ, an imprint of HarperCollins*Publishers* Ltd in 2024

HB ISBN: 9780008580117
PB ISBN: 9780008580131

This book is produced from independently certified FSC™ paper
to ensure responsible forest management.

For more information visit: www.harpercollins.co.uk/green

Printed and Bound in the UK using 100% Renewable Electricity at
CPI Group (UK) Ltd, Croydon, CR0 4YY

Disclaimer from the authors: Our Heartbreak Hotel clients are our top priority,
and their confidences are safely guarded. Therefore, we have created fictionalised
portraits of retreat attendees to portray the types of challenges and revelations that
might surface but in no way factually report actual encounters.